W9-CUJ-334

**ARE YOU CARRYING ANY GOLD
OR LIVING RELATIVES?**

BY IRENE KAMPEN

ARE YOU CARRYING ANY GOLD
OR LIVING RELATIVES?

DUE TO LACK OF INTEREST
TOMORROW HAS BEEN CANCELED

HERE COMES THE BRIDE,
THERE GOES MOTHER

LAST YEAR AT SUGARBUSH

EUROPE WITHOUT GEORGE

THE ZIEGFELDS' GIRL
(*With Patricia Ziegfeld and Suzanne Gleaves*)

WE THAT ARE LEFT

LIFE WITHOUT GEORGE

Are You Carrying
Any Gold
or Living Relatives?
by Irene Kampen

Doubleday & Company, Inc., Garden City, New York
1970

A1-733 641

Library of Congress Catalog Card Number 70–111169
Copyright © 1970 by Irene Kampen
All Rights Reserved
Printed in the United States of America
First Edition

For
Robert Magidoff

ARE YOU CARRYING ANY GOLD
OR LIVING RELATIVES?

CHAPTER ONE

I cannot forecast to you the action of Russia. It is a riddle wrapped in a mystery inside an enigma.

Winston Churchill

It sounded to me like a harebrained scheme from the very beginning so right away I said, "No, I don't want to go to the Soviet Union with you, Nila."

But even as I was saying it I knew, in the pit of my stomach, that I was going to end up in the Soviet Union with Nila. Ever since I was a little tiny girl I have been saying, "No, I don't want to" to people, as in "No, I don't want to go to kindergarten today" and "No, I don't want to subscribe to the *Reader's Digest*" and "No, I don't want to get divorced" and "No, I don't want to learn to ski" and I have ended up doing every single one of them, especially learning to ski, during which I broke my left ankle last winter at a place called Magic Mountain in Vermont.

"And look how you are still limping," Nila said to me. "When we get to the Soviet Union we will turn ourselves into a sanatorium and the doctors will make your ankle so strong you will end up dancing in the Bolshoi Ballet!"

"I don't want to turn myself into a sanatorium in the Soviet Union," I said.

Nila took the Intourist Travel booklet out of her purse and said, "Imagine! For the first time in history the Soviets are opening their roads to foreign tourists!"

"Oh, are they really?" I said, trying to sound as though I was even faintly interested in what the Soviets were doing with their roads. "Imagine!"

"We will rent a Russian car," Nila said, "and we will drive south through the Caucasus Mountains." "I don't want to drive through the Caucasus Mountains," I said.

"We will camp along the way," Nila said. "Just the two of us. Imagine!—singing and laughing, day and night!" "I don't want to camp along the way," I said.

"Such an adventure!" Nila said. "How you can say 'No' to such an adventure?"

I must explain that Nila is Russian-born and was an anti-Stalinist and was thrown into Lubyanka Prison in Moscow and later exiled to Siberia. She had to walk about five hundred miles through the snow across Siberia.

Eventually she married an NBC correspondent and became an American citizen but still, when Nila says "What an adventure!" it is not the same thing as you or I saying "What an adventure!" It is very frightening, especially because Nila loved the Siberian countryside.

"Siberia was beautiful!" Nila says as she reminisces about those dear old days. "So clean! The air so fresh! The sky so blue! The snow so white!"

So you can imagine how I felt. "No, I don't want to go camping with you in the Soviet Union, Nila," I said again.

"We will fish in beautiful Lake Sevan in Armenia," Nila said. She found the place in the Intourist booklet where it tells how the Soviets are simply longing for foreign tourists to come over and fish in beautiful Lake Sevan, highest lake in the world, and how they will also throw in a guide and a tent and fishing equipment for only seven rubles a day.

"How they can do this so cheap?" Nila marveled.

"How much is a ruble?" I asked.

"Ruble is worth one dollar ten cents in American money," Nila said. "We will fish, we will cruise across the Black Sea, we will rest and take cure in sanatorium, we will laugh, we will sing—my, how we will sing!" And Nila began to sing, quite loudly, in Russian.

At the moment we were sitting at the counter of a Chock Full O'Nuts Restaurant on Fifty-seventh Street in New York City, but when Nila gets the urge to sing, or to dance or to cry for that matter, she goes right ahead with it. I suppose walking five hundred miles across Siberia gets rid of any little inhibitions a person might otherwise have about carrying on in public.

"I don't want to go to the Soviet Union, Nila," I said, when she had finished singing.

"That was famous Russian song about love and war," Nila told me (also the man on the stool next to us and the counter girls and the manager who came out of the kitchen to see what the hell was going on in his restaurant). "Song tells story of Cossack soldier who goes to fight for Tsar and leaves young wife behind. Wife tries to swim across river after him and drowns."

Nila took a handkerchief out of her purse and mopped her eyes. "Very sad song," she said. "My friend here and I are going to Russia this summer," she told the man on the stool and the counter girls and the manager. "We

11

are going to camp and fish and sing and laugh day and night like two mads!"

"I'm going to the Soviet Union this summer," I told Dr. Howard. Dr. Howard is a great big important orthopedic specialist in Connecticut and he and I had been seeing a lot of each other since that magic moment when I fell down Magic Mountain and broke my ankle.

"Why are you going to the Soviet Union?" Dr. Howard asked. I told him that the Soviets were opening their roads to foreign tourists for the first time and how Nila and I were going to rent a car and drive all over Russia.

"We're going to camp and fish and sail across the Black Sea," I said, "and sing a lot," I added.

"Hmmm," Dr. Howard said.

"And we're going to a sanatorium to take the cure," I said. "The cure for what?" Dr. Howard wanted to know.

I thought for a minute. "I don't exactly know," I said.

"The whole project sounds like a harebrained scheme to me," Dr. Howard said.

"You have pencil?" Nila said to me on the phone. "Good. Write this down—Visa. Passport. International Driver's License. Five passport photographs. Put everything in an envelope and mail to Bloomingdale's."

Bloomingdale's is a New York City department store. "Why should I mail it to Bloomingdale's?" I asked.

"In Bloomingdale's is American Express office which arranges trip," Nila explained. "In American Express office is Denise Daverre who takes care all my travel arrangements."

Nila travels a lot because she lectures to women's clubs

about Russia. "Denise is lovely French girl," Nila told me.

I frankly was not too crazy about the idea of a lovely French girl in Bloomingdale's arranging a tour of Russia for me but I kept my doubts to myself. With Nila it is sometimes wiser not to express your doubts aloud in order to avoid long emotional discussions of the situation (or as is usually the case with Nila, the Situation).

"I have just mailed you wonderful gift from Bloomingdale's," Nila said. "And now, my dearest friend, I say good-bye. Across the miles between us I embrace you. Soon, if heaven should only hear my prayers, we will meet once more."

This is how Nila ordinarily says good-bye at the end of a telephone conversation. If you should happen to be parting from her in person, especially if you are going somewhere out of state like New Jersey, it takes a good ten minutes to say good-bye to her. First you have to sit down in silence and compose your thoughts (old Russian custom) and then you have to kiss each other on both cheeks and say things like "May the saints in heaven watch over your footsteps" and "Let nothing but omens of good fortune attend your journey" and "Go, with God."

Nila's gift arrived the next day. The mailman had to bring it to the door because it was too big to fit into the mailbox. It was an album of records.

RUSSIAN IN A NUTSHELL the label read; LEARN RUSSIAN IN RECORD TIME. Inside the album were four long-playing records and a phrase book also entitled *Russian in a Nutshell.*

"Simply follow the conversations on the record in your phrase book," the instructions said, "and you will pick up the Russian language easily and fluently by listening and talking, just the way you learned English as a child."

My record player was back at its factory somewhere in Pennsylvania being repaired so I went up to the attic and found my daughter Christine's old record player and brought it downstairs. My mother had given the machine to Chris for Chris's third birthday. There was a record still on the turntable. I took it off and read the label. It was *Here Comes Peter Cottontail* (flip side, *Three Blind Mice*).

I put side one of RUSSIAN IN A NUTSHELL on the turntable and started the machine. First I heard some unidentifiable squawks and scratches, followed by what sounded like somebody shouting at me in Yiddish through a child's sand strainer.

I turned off the machine and drove downtown and bought myself another record player. I now owned three record players, which is the way things often turn out when Nila does something wonderful for you.

I turned on the new record player. "How you do?" a deep Slavic voice said. "My name is Professor Matkovsky. Together you and I going to learn how to speak beautiful Russian language. Open book, kindly."

I opened *Russian in a Nutshell.*

"We begin with basic conversational words and phrases," Professor Matkovsky said. "Ready?" "Ready," I said.

"Repeat after me," Professor Matkovsky said. "Ya n'i-pa-n'i MA-yu pa-RU-sk'i."

"Ya n'i-pa-n'i MA-yu pa-RU-sk'i," I repeated. I looked it up in *Russian in a Nutshell.* It meant "I do not under-

14

stand Russian." "Well, God knows that's true, Professor Matkovsky," I said.

"YA ha-CHU S'EST," Professor Matkovsky said. "YA ha-CHU S'EST" I said. "YA n'i ha-CHU S'EST," the professor said. "You're going too fast," I said. "I'm still looking up—" "SUP p'i-r'i-SO-l'in," Professor Matkovsky said. "I-VAN BU-d'it ZAF-tra-kat. E-ta MOZH-na. E-ta PRA-v'il-na. Ya n'i—"

"You're going too fast!" I said. I lifted the tone arm and started the record over again.

"How you do?" Professor Matkovsky said. "My name is Professor Matkovsky. Together you and I going to learn how to speak beautiful Russian language."

The dog has a perfect set of human vocal chords but cannot speak because it does not have the mental ability to memorize a series of sounds in sequence.

Scientific American Magazine

"No, I don't want to take a Polaroid camera with me to Russia, George," I said. I was spending the weekend with George and his wife at their summer home outside of Boston.

"Of course you want to take a Polaroid camera with you," George said.

"No, I don't," I said. "I'm carrying about a million pieces of baggage as it is and besides I don't know how to use a Polaroid camera. Thank you very much, though."

"I'll teach you how to use it," George said. George is an executive vice-president of the Polaroid Corporation of America and the way he got to be executive vice-president was by never taking *no* for an answer.

"You'll thank me when you get to the Soviet Union," George said. "The Russians love to have their photographs taken. They're like children when it comes to the Polaroid camera."

It developed almost at once that the Russians aren't the only ones who are like children when it comes to the Polaroid camera.

"Wrong again," George told me. "You're holding the camera sideways. See that little square in the lens? If you frame the subject's face in that square you can't go wrong. Try again." I tried again.

"I don't understand," George said. "This camera was designed so that even an idiot can work it. Try once more." I tried once more.

"No, no, no!" George said. "You've got your thumb over the lens." "Which is the lens?" I asked. "It's the thing you've got your thumb over!" George said. I took my thumb off the lens.

"You are now holding the camera upside down," George said tonelessly. I turned the camera around and something on the back fell open. "Now you're holding it inside out!" George cried. "Good God!"

He grabbed the camera away from me. For the executive vice-president of a corporation employing nine thousand people in the Boston area alone George seemed to be going to pieces fairly rapidly.

"I'll practice with the camera, George," I said, in an attempt to calm him down. "Let me try one more of you—stand over there against the stone wall."

George went across the lawn and stood against the stone wall. I followed him. "Stand absolutely still," I told him. "Be sure and get my head centered in the square," he said. I snapped the picture.

"Let's see it," George said. I handed it to him. "What do you think?" I said.

"I think it's the lousiest picture I have ever laid my eyes on in the course of my entire career with Polaroid," George said. "I'm only grateful that Edwin Land, the inventor of the camera, isn't here to see it."

I took the picture back and studied it. "I don't think it's so bad," I said, "outside of the fact that you came out orange."

Two days later the mailman rang my doorbell again. This time it was a carton containing fifty packages of Polaroid color film, compliments of George.

I went up to the attic and found another suitcase. My baggage now consisted of three suitcases, one hang-up garment bag, a Pan-American flight bag, a Polaroid camera in its carrying case, and a Fun Fur coat.

The coat was Bloomingdale's fault. "I'm looking for a warm, practical coat," I told the saleslady. I couldn't resist adding, "To wear in Russia."

"Russia?" the saleslady exclaimed. "How exciting! Let me tell our coat buyer, Mr. Grayson—he'll be so interested." She trotted off and returned with Mr. Grayson.

"Miss McGiven tells me you're going to Russia," Mr. Grayson said. "What a thrilling journey that will be!" (Mr. Grayson was a bit wispy.) "We must send you off in something smashing," he said. "Honor of the U.S.A. and all that, you know." He frowned in thought for a moment and then his face lit up. "I know the very thing for you!" he said. "A Fun Fur!"

"Well, what I really had in mind was something in navy blue—" I began, but Mr. Grayson said, "No, no, navy blue is for schoolgirls. With your height you can carry

17

something really *different*. Miss McGiven, bring out that new number that just came into the stockroom."

Miss McGiven trotted off again. When she returned this time she was carrying in her arms what appeared to be a dead St. Bernard.

"I just know you'll be crazy mad for this," Mr. Grayson told me. Miss McGiven handed him the St. Bernard, which turned out on closer inspection to be a brown and white Borgana Fun Fur. "Here," Mr. Grayson said. "Slip into this."

I slipped into it.

"Stunning!" Mr. Grayson said. "Simply stunning! It's definitely *you*—am I right, Miss McGiven?"

Miss McGiven said he was right, it was definitely me. I looked at my reflection in the mirror. "What kind of fur is this supposed to be?" I asked.

Mr. Grayson said what difference did it make, the point was that it was *fun!*

"Well," I said dubiously. I turned around and looked at myself in the mirror from the back. "It seems awfully big," I said.

"Just right for those nippy Moscow nights," Mr. Grayson assured me. "Oh, you *must* take it—I insist. You'll be an absolute sensation in Russia in your Fun Fur!"

It was Sunday morning of the day we were scheduled to fly to Moscow via Pan American Airlines. I turned on the radio to listen to the weather report.

"Pan American Airlines is on strike," the news announcer said. "All Pan-American passengers holding confirmed reservations are requested to call this special number—Watkins 5-4342—for further information."

I dialed Watkins 5-4342. "Pan Am makes the going

18

great!" a voice informed me. "Pan American Airlines is on strike."

"I know," I said. "What are we supposed—"

"Pan-American passengers holding confirmed reservations are requested to call Watkins 5-4342 for further information," the voice said.

"This *is* Watkins 5-4342," I said. "What's the idea of—"

"Pan Am makes the going great!" the voice said. "Pan American Airlines is on strike. Pan-American passengers holding con—"

I hung up and called Bloomingdale's. Bloomingdale's was closed. I called Nila. Nobody answered. I went into the spare room where my luggage was piled up. "Pan American Airlines is on strike," I told the luggage.

The telephone rang. I picked it up. "Pan Am makes the going great!" a voice said. "This is Pan American Airlines."

"Are you a recorded voice or are you a person?" I said.

"I am a person, naturally," Pan American said, offended.

"Well, what am I supposed to do about my flight to Moscow?" I asked.

"The airline is arranging alternate flights for all our passengers," Pan American said. "Hold yourself in readiness. We will call you back." He hung up.

I went into the spare room again and found the suitcase with the emergency bag in it and took out the bottle of tranquilizers. The telephone rang again.

"This is Aunt Birdie calling," Aunt Birdie told me. "Pan American Airlines is on strike." "I know," I said. "I only hope it's not an evil omen," Aunt Birdie said.

"I can't talk now, Aunt Birdie," I said. "Pan American may be trying to call me."

"Promise me you won't forget to look up Cousin Masha

when you get to Odessa," Aunt Birdie said. "She isn't actually your cousin, of course—she's Vaclav Pinman's niece. His oldest sister's grandchild, that is."

"I'll try and look her up, Aunt Birdie," I said. "I really have to hang up now because—"

"I still don't understand why you're going to Russia," Aunt Birdie said. "It sounds like a harebrained scheme to me. Look what happened to poor Cousin Masha. Vaclav took the whole family back for a visit when Masha was fifteen and that was the last anyone saw of Masha. She fell in love with a sailor in Odessa and that was the end. Good-bye, Masha."

"I know," I said. "I honestly have to hang—"

"Vaclav was always a fool," Aunt Birdie said, and hung up. The phone rang again almost immediately.

"Pan Am makes the going great!" a voice said. "Pan American Airlines is on strike."

I gritted my teeth. "I already know that," I said.

"We have made alternate arrangements for you to fly to Moscow at six P.M. tonight," the voice said. "Via Finnair."

"Via what?" I said. "Finnair," Pan American said. "Thin air?" I said.

"FINN!" Pan American said. "F as in Fatal, I as in Iceberg, double N as in Never-Never. Finnair!"

RUSSIAN IN A NUTSHELL

Useful Phrases

I am an American.
Ya a-m'i-r'i KA-nska.

I do not want to sit down.

ARE YOU CARRYING ANY GOLD OR LIVING RELATIVES?
Ya n'i ha-CHU S'EST.

This soup is oversalted.
SUP p'i-r'i-SO-l'in.

Yes.
Da.

No.
Nyet.

I do not understand Russian.
Ya n'i pa-n'i-MA-yu pa-RU-sk'i.

CHAPTER TWO

To travel hopefully is a better thing than to arrive.

Robert Louis Stevenson

"Russians think all American tourists are rich," Nila explained to me as we flew eastward on the last leg of our flight from New York to Moscow via Helsinki, Finland.

A beautiful Finnish stewardess poured champagne and served us black Russian caviar on wafer-thin slices of Swedish bread.

"The more rich you behave the happier Russian people will be," Nila said to me. A second stewardess appeared with a fresh bottle of champagne. Hot on her heels came a third stewardess who presented Nila and me with furry slippers, French perfume, satin sleep masks, and Finnish chocolates. "Courtesy of Finnair," the stewardess said.

"Also remember never to wear slacks in Soviet Union," Nila told me. "No slacks, and no scarf around head. When President Roosevelt's daughter-in-law visited Moscow she dressed in plain clothes and wore babushka, and Russian women were very insulted. They thought she was trying to look like peasant."

A handsome blond Finnish purser in a turtle-neck

sweater and tailored slacks asked us if we would prefer
Steak Chateaubriand or Poached Filet of Sole Archduke
for dinner.

"And perhaps another glass of champagne?" he said.
"Brandy? Liqueur? Pillows? Blankets? Music? Sibelius?
Motion pictures? French pastry? Turkish cigarettes?"

"Say 'Yes' to everything," Nila advised me, "because
when we get to Soviet Union will be nobody giving away
perfume and French pastry, this I absolutely guarantee.
We will be lucky if we even have sink stopper in hotel
bathroom."

"In that case I won't be able to look very rich," I said.
"Rich people take baths. It's impossible to take a bath
in a bathtub with no sink stopper."

"You will learn," Nila said.

The plane began its descent to the Moscow airport.
I drew aside the window curtain and looked out for my
first glimpse of the green Russian countryside.

"It looks just like Michigan," an American tourist behind me said.

"Who this person?" Moscow Airport Customs Control
demanded. He was looking at my passport photograph.

"Why, that's me," I said. Customs Control examined
the photograph through narrowed eyes and said something in Russian.

"What did he say?" I asked Nila. "Never mind," Nila
said. "You wouldn't like."

Customs Control returned my passport and demanded
to know whether I was carrying any gold, silver, jewelry,
or living relatives into the Soviet Union. He wrote a lot
of things down on an official-looking piece of paper,
stamped it, and presented it to me.

"Very important document," Nila told me. "If you lose this the Soviets will not allow you to leave the country at end of our trip." I put the very important document away in my passport folder behind my smallpox certificate. "Now we collect our baggage and take taxicab into city of Moscow," she said.

We found our baggage heaped up next to the exit. "My God, what you got there?" Nila said.

"It's a Fun Fur coat," I said.

"We not going to Siberia, you know," Nila said. We got into a taxicab. "First thing we will do is go to Moscow Intourist office and arrange everything for start of our journey tomorrow," Nila said to me. She tapped the driver on the shoulder. "Hotel Russia," she told him.

The drive from the airport took about forty minutes. It was a sunny August day and the countryside was so pastoral it was difficult to believe that we were approaching a city the size of Moscow. All around us we saw meadows and woodlands and flowers. Many families were picnicking by the side of the road.

The transition from country to suburbs was so gradual that before I knew it we had left the meadows and woods behind and were driving along a broad highway divided by a grass mall. The first apartment houses appeared. Giant derricks loomed against the skyline. Traffic became heavier. Taxicab drivers leaned on their horns and shouted imprecations out the windows of their cabs at each other just the way taxicab drivers do back in dear old New York City.

On every block great arches had been erected spanning the central mall. The arches were decorated with huge photographs of Lenin surmounted by the hammer and sickle motif and bearing the letters "CCCP" along with a legend in Russian.

"Means 'Hail to the glorious Communist Party,'" Nila translated. "Entire nation is preparing to celebrate birthday of Lenin next year."

"I thought Lenin was dead," I said.

"Lenin is dead," Nila said. "That's reason they celebrating his birthday."

We stopped for a traffic light. A line of Muscovites was queued up at a sidewalk stand where a man in a white apron was selling ice-cream cones. Two women in shapeless cotton summer dresses stood waiting at a bus stop. An old woman in cracked boots and with a babushka on her head swept the gutter with a straw broom.

"Look—there is a Red Army General," Nila told me, pointing at a bemedaled officer standing on the curb. A black limousine drew up and the general opened its rear door and climbed in. The limousine drove off, right through the red traffic light. The car's back window was daintily curtained in white organdy.

"Whenever you see automobile with curtains on window you can be sure that inside is riding a very important person," Nila told me.

The light had turned green and traffic was moving once more. "Here we are at Hotel Russia," Nila said.

"Good grief!" I said. The Hotel Russia was enormous.

"Biggest hotel in Europe," Nila said. "Brand new. Five thousand rooms." She opened the door of the taxicab. "Don't forget what I told you on airplane," she cautioned me. "Look very rich."

We presented ourselves at the Moscow Intourist office

26

in the Hotel Russia to make arrangements for our camping trip.

"Impossible," Moscow Intourist said.

"What you mean, 'impossible'?" Nila said.

"I mean impossible," Intourist said. "Person who can help you is home today, resting. Come back tomorrow."

"Tomorrow we already supposed to be on our way to camp at Podolsk," Nila said. Intourist said, "Podolsk is closed," and disappeared into an inner office.

"Citizen!" Nila called after him. "We are guests in your country!" She hammered on the counter. "Is this how you treat guests in the Soviet Union?"

Intourist reappeared. "What you want from me?" Intourist demanded. "Why you are banging and yelling like a mad?"

"I tell you what we want from you," Nila said. "We want vouchers for renting car and gasoline and camping and food coupons which we already paid in United States of America nearly three thousand dollars each for, that's what we want from you."

Intourist fished around under the counter and came up with a stack of papers. "Name?" he said to Nila.

"Magidoff and Kampen," Nila said. Intourist thumbed through the papers and said, "Not here. Come back tomorrow."

"Citizen," Nila said, "I assure you we not only here but we here for eight-week trip." She took a copy of our itinerary out of her purse and gave it to Intourist. "Look!" she said.

"What this document?" Intourist inquired, holding the itinerary gingerly.

"Itinerary for trip," Nila said. "From Bloomingdale's."

Intourist examined the itinerary, scowling, while Nila

drummed on the countertop and I tried to look rich. The office was rapidly filling up with tourists—Germans, French, some Finns, a few Americans—all crying, as in one voice, for cars, drivers, guides, and the Bolshoi Ballet. The word "voucher," sometimes pronounced "woucher" or "wouch" was uttered at frequent intervals, as in "Where is your wouch?" or "This is wrong wouch!"

Intourist handed the itinerary back to Nila and said, "Impossible," again.

"You can see for yourself," Intourist said, "itinerary calls for first stop at Podolsk. Podolsk is closed to foreign tourists."

"So we will drive to Orel instead and make first stop there," Nila said. "Now be so kind as to give us vouchers and coupons for Orel camp."

"After you give me ten dollars additional payment," Intourist said. "American money, be so kind."

"For what reason I'm supposed to give you ten dollars?" Nila inquired. Intourist said ten dollars was the standard penalty charged by Intourist for modification of an itinerary.

"You supposed to camp first night at Podolsk," Intourist said. "Instead you going to Orel. Change in itinerary? Change in itinerary. Ten dollars."

"Orel?" Intourist Rent-A-Car said, looking at our itinerary. "You plan to drive on first day to Orel?" Intourist Rent-A-Car, located in the Hotel Metropole, was a young man named Vladimir and his elderly assistant, Boris, who trembled.

"Yes, we plan to drive on first day to Orel," Nila told Vladimir. Vladimir turned to Boris and spoke to him in

Russian. "Vladimir is explaining itinerary to Boris," Nila told me.

"Orel?" Boris said, when Vladimir had finished explaining. He rolled his eyes heavenward. "Oy," he said.

"What's the matter?" I said. I was beginning to experience the old sinking sensation in the pit of my stomach. "What's wrong with Orel?" I asked Vladimir.

"For two ladies to drive alone to Orel is terrible undertaking," Vladimir told me.

"Is nothing," Nila said scornfully. "In United States of America ladies drive alone all the time. What is difficulty? You get in car, you push button, and zoom! you drive. Nothing to it."

"What button?" Vladimir asked.

"Button you push to make car go," Nila told him.

"In Soviet Union is no button to push," Vladimir said.

"What you mean?" Nila said. "How you make car go?"

Vladimir said a word that sounded like "*stsyeplyehnee-yeh.*" "I don't know this word," Nila told him. Vladimir acted out an elaborate pantomime of shifting gears.

"He means a car with a clutch and a stick shift," I told Nila.

"I don't know how to drive such a car," Nila told Vladimir. "In United States of America I drive Buick with automatic shift. In Buick a person gets in, a person pushes the button, a person drives. Be so kind as to rent us car with automatic shift."

"In Soviet Union is no car with automatic shift," Vladimir said.

"Nila," I said, "are you saying that you do not know how to drive a standard-shift car?"

"Absolutely," Nila said. "Never learned such a thing. You know how to drive such a car?"

"Yes," I said, numbly.

"Good!" Nila said. "In that case you will drive and I will read maps and road signs. Perfect!"

"Nila," I said, "unfortunately it is not going to be possible for me to drive a strange foreign car in a strange foreign country for three thousand miles, especially since the clutch pedal is on the left and my left ankle was recently in a cast."

"Of course is not possible, darling," Nila said. "You will drive only to Orel, and at the Orel camp we will hire driver for rest of trip."

"How do you know there's going to be a driver to hire at the Orel camp?" I said.

"We find one," Nila assured me. "Will be marvelous— what an adventure!" She turned to Vladimir. "Please show us car now," she said.

Vladimir and Boris led us out to the parking lot. "Here is car," Vladimir said. "Volga 21."

I studied the Volga 21 from all angles. It looked like the old Mercury used to look, only smaller.

"You like the car?" Vladimir asked me.

Instead of answering him I asked, "Where are the windshield wipers?"

Vladimir said the windshield wipers were hidden under the front seat and must be attached to the windshield only when Nila and I were physically present in the car owing to a rash of windshield-wiper robberies that had recently broken out in the Soviet Union.

"I will explain to you how car works," Vladimir said. We all climbed into the Volga and Vladimir proceeded to warn me that the car must be measured daily for water and oil and must be kept immaculately clean at all times

30

because in Russia it is a misdemeanor to be caught driving a dirty car.

"You can be arrested by Militiaman and fined ten rubles," he said. "Militiaman is Soviet policeman."

Next Vladimir pointed out to me where the choke was located and where the spare tire was and where the spare-tire jack was. ("Never in my life I heard anything so crazy!" Nila kept muttering under her breath. "In America a person gets into car, a person pushes the button, a person drives away!")

Vladimir also explained to me how to change the oil, add the water, clean the carburetor, put out the fire, and a few other little chores which might crop up during our journey. All this time Boris was in the back seat, trembling.

"Road map is in glove compartment," Vladimir said. "I advise you not to take road map too seriously because map has very little connection with actual situation on road."

"I have marvelous idea!" Nila cried suddenly. "Oy," I said. "While we all right here in parking lot I will take driving lesson and learn to drive this car," Nila said. "Boris will teach."

Boris began to tremble harder than ever. "Not to worry," Nila assured Boris. "I am fast learner. I learned English language in only three weeks, imagine!"

Vladimir and I went back inside the hotel to fill out some very important documents concerning the car rental. After about fifteen minutes Nila and Boris appeared. Boris was shaking like an aspen.

"Impossible to learn to drive such a car!" Nila told Vladimir crossly. "In America is nothing to drive a car —push the button, go! Child could learn."

31

She turned to me. "Take Polaroid of Boris and give him for souvenir," she said.

I took Polaroid of Boris. He turned out gray.

"You want to take excursion to Kremlin this afternoon?" Nila asked me.

"I can't," I said. "I'm studying."

"What you studying?" Nila said.

"I'm studying for our trip tomorrow," I said.

RUSSIAN IN A NUTSHELL

Difficulties on the Road

Our car is stuck in (the mud) the snow.
Hahsg ahf-tuh-mah-BEEL azhs-TRYAHL (ugryah-ZEE) fsnyeh-GOO.

How far is the nearest town?
Kahk dah-lyeh-KAW dah blee-AHAH-Y-sheh-vuh GAW-ruh-dah?

A puncture.
Prah-Kawl.

A slow leak.
MYED-lyen-nah-yah oo-TYECH-kah.

Something (rattles) knocks.
SHTAW-tuh (dryeh-byeh-AHEET) stoo-CHEET.

We had just finished dinner. Nila said, "Now I will explain to you how to use coupons because during our trip we must pay for everything in Intourist coupons, understand?"

"No," I said.

"We have blue coupons for breakfast, pink coupons for lunch, green coupons—oh, my God!"

32

"What's the matter?" I asked. Nila was scrabbling frantically around in her purse. "What *is* it?" I said.

"I lost!" she cried. "You lost what?" I asked. "Very important document," Nila said.

"Which one?" I asked. Nila said very important document issued this afternoon by Intourist and giving us official permission to travel up, down, and possibly sideways on the roads of the Soviet Union.

"Can't we get another one?" I asked.

"We cannot only not get another one," Nila told me tragically, "but without original document we will be forced to cancel entire trip and return home at once to United States of America."

"Gosh, what a shame," I said, trying to mask my sudden elation at this glorious bit of news. "I don't want you to blame yourself, Nila—it just wasn't meant to be. Maybe next year."

"I find!" Nila cried happily. She produced the very important document from the depths of her pocketbook. "Thanks God I found," she said. "Here—you keep it. Put it in passport case."

I put it into my passport case. While I had my pocketbook open I took out my pillbox.

"Imagine!" Nila said. "By this time tomorrow night we will be already sleeping in tents under the stars at the Orel camp. We will be laughing and singing around campfire with new Russian friends." She looked at me. "You are not excited?" she asked.

"Oh my, yes, I'm terribly excited," I said. "It's just that I wish—"

"What you wish?" Nila demanded.

"Nothing," I said. I opened the pillbox and took out a tranquilizer.

33

"Why you are taking pill?" Nila asked.

"Because I'm so excited," I said.

"What did I do wrong?" I asked Nila in fright. It was bright and early the next morning. We had scarcely left the suburbs of Moscow behind when a Militiaman leaped out of the bushes, brandishing his baton at us like Leonard Bernstein conducting the *Eroica*. Militiamen in Russia are dressed like Red Army soldiers, or enough like Red Army soldiers to give a person heart failure.

"Stop the car!" Nila told me. I slammed on the brakes. The Militiaman stuck his head through the window and shouted something in Russian. "*Ya ni panimayu Paruski,*" I told him in a quavering voice.

"Militiaman demands your passport," Nila informed me. "Also visa, international driver's license, gas coupons, and very important document from Intourist."

I handed everything over. "What did I do wrong?" I said to Nila. "It must have been something terrible."

"I will ask," Nila said. She asked the Militiaman in Russian what I had done wrong. He answered her. "You ran over Soviet chicken," Nila informed me.

"I never even saw it," I said. "Do you think he's going to arrest us?"

"Who cares?" Nila said. "So we arrested—so what? Will be adventure. I already arrested so many times in this country I lost count."

The Militiaman was now writing things down in a black notebook. "Take Polaroid of him," Nila said to me. "We will present it as souvenir from America."

I got out of the car and took a Polaroid of the Militiaman. I was shaking so hard I could scarcely hold the camera.

"I explain to Militiaman how camera works while you

develop picture," Nila said. She explained to him. "Militiaman wishes to know how much such a camera costs in
America," she said to me.

"About thirty-five dollars," I said.

"Costs two hundred dollars," Nila told the Militiaman.
"More expensive sounds better," she explained to me.
"He very much impressed."

I gave the two-hundred-dollar photograph to the Militiaman along with a ten-ruble fine for running over the
chicken. The Militiaman returned all my documents and
waved us on with a smile full of gold teeth.

"Very nice Militiaman," Nila said to me. "Friendly,
like a child."

We drove on. "It's starting to rain," I said after a few
minutes. I pulled over to the side of the road and stopped
the car. "We'd better put on the windshield wipers," I
said.

"Won't be necessary," Nila told me. "Now it begins
to sleet. Windshield is freezing over—see?" The sky had
turned black and lightning was ripping across the
horizon.

"My!" Nila said. "And now is falling down on the roof
—what is English word for what is falling down on roof?"

"Hailstones," I said bitterly.

"Ah!" Nila said. "Hailstones. Strange word. Couldn't
remember."

It was rapidly becoming obvious that somebody up
there was trying to tell me something and had indeed
been attempting to get through to me for a long time,
beginning at ten o'clock in the morning on March 18
at Magic Mountain, Vermont, where I had broken my
ankle.

"Nila," I said, "I think that the time has come for us

35

to take an impartial look at the situation and decide whether to turn back before it's too late."

"Turn back?" Nila said. "Why you want to turn back? We just started."

"I want to turn back because I'm afraid," I said. "I'm not as brave as you are."

"What you afraid of?" Nila demanded.

"Everything," I said. "The storm. This automobile. The Militiaman. The Caucasus Mountains. The Communist Party. Lenin."

"Lenin is dead," Nila said. She patted my arm. "Poor darling, it has been terrible day for you," she said in sympathy. "I promise that tonight when we arrive at Orel camp I will manage everything—I will pitch our tent, I will fix you soft bed under stars, I will cook you fluffy omelet over campfire."

"Car needs gas," Nila announced. The storm had died down and we were once more driving toward Orel. So far since leaving Moscow we had not passed a single gas station. "Here is station now!" Nila said. "Just in time."

I stopped the car next to the lone gas pump.

"After we get gas we will go into café and have good hot meal," Nila said. "Maybe we will drink glass of wine, make friends with Russian people—everything will be marvelous."

We waited in the rain for about five minutes. Nothing happened. "When will everything start getting marvelous?" I inquired.

Nila went into the station office to investigate the situation. She returned looking thoughtful. The gas station situation in the Soviet Union, she reported, was as follows:

There are no friendly uniformed attendants to pump the gas into the car, measure the oil, check the battery, add the water, wipe the windshield, or put air into the tires. The driver performs all these operations himself. (*Citizens of the USSR have the right to work.* Joseph Stalin.)

To come right down to it, there are no attendants whatsoever, friendly or unfriendly. What there is is a cross old woman who takes the gas coupons and she doesn't come out into the rain to do it either. (*Citizens of the USSR have the right to rest.* Ibid.)

"Come into office with me and bring gas coupons," Nila said. "When cross old woman sees how rich you look she will maybe find us nice Soviet gentleman to help pump gas into car."

I trailed after Nila to the office through the rain. Nila paused at the office doorway and studied me with a critical eye.

"You don't look as rich as you looked when we were in Moscow," she said. She frowned at my sodden appearance. "Put on blue sunglasses," she told me.

"If I walk in wearing blue sunglasses in the rain this woman will think I'm crazy," I said.

"Rich and crazy," Nila said, nodding. "Marvelous combination."

I put on the blue sunglasses. The office was empty except for the old woman who was reclining in a scarred leather armchair and sipping a steaming glass of tea. The minute we walked in she lowered the glass and said "*Nyet!*" at us. She pronounced it exactly the way Professor Matkovsky had pronounced it on *Russian in a Nutshell*, with a sort of growl in the middle.

"*Benzin?*" Nila said.

37

"*Nyet!*" the old woman said again. It dawned on me that this was something of a historic moment. I had just heard and understood my first all-Russian conversation— an accomplishment which had been one of the professor's fondest dreams for me. It wasn't much of a conversation, but still—

"I gather that there's no gasoline," I said to Nila. "As I understood the conversation, when you asked this woman for gasoline she told you that there was no gasoline, correct?"

"You understood conversation!" Nila said approvingly. "Very good!" The old woman let loose with a flood of Russian. "You understood that too?" Nila asked me.

"Well, no," I said. "Not really."

"She says that gasoline truck may arrive from Moscow in hour or so," Nila said. "She also says that on the other hand gasoline truck may not arrive."

The old woman said something else. "What did she say this time?" I asked Nila.

"She asks whether you have any American chewing gum to give her," Nila said. "Answer her in Russian—will please her."

"*Nyet*," I said to the old woman.

"Very good," Nila said again. "And while we wait for gas truck we will go into café and eat good hot lunch."

"This is what you consider a good hot lunch?" I said to Nila. We were in the station café, which was incredibly smelly, and Nila had gone to the serving counter to get us some food.

"Nothing else left in kitchen," Nila said.

"What's that?" I asked, pointing to a glass of something

38

that looked like a mixture of curdled buttermilk and library paste.

"Kefir," Nila said. "Very healthy Russian beverage. Have some."

"No thank you," I said. I ate a piece of stale black bread and washed it down with some murky water. "If Dr. Safford back in Connecticut could see me drinking this water he would be like a mad," I said.

I stood up. "I'm going to the ladies' room," I said.

"I sincerely don't advise," Nila told me. I went anyway. When I came back Nila took one look at the expression on my face and said, "Well, I warned."

She finished her Kefir. "Never mind," she comforted me, "bathroom situation was much worse in Siberia."

The gas truck from Moscow arrived at last and we reached the outskirts of Orel at sunset. Ominous noises were coming from under the hood of the Volga 21. "Something rattles," I told Nila.

"Camp can't be too far away now," Nila said. (She had been saying this at half-hour intervals ever since we left Moscow.) She looked at me anxiously. "You are going to cry?" she asked.

"I'm just tired," I said. She patted my arm again.

"Courage!" she said. "In a few minutes you will be laughing and singing and eating a fluffy omelet, I promise you. See—here is sign for Orel camp at last. We are here!"

I drove through the camp gates and stopped the car. Nila and I peered out through the rain-spattered windshield. Nila was the first to speak.

"Must be some terrible mistake," she said.

CHAPTER THREE

This will last out a night in Russia,
When nights are longest there.

William Shakespeare

How to describe the Orel camp?

If someone were to take an abandoned Fort Dix barracks, peel off all the exterior paint, break a few of its windows, and set it down in a sea of mud in Russia they would have the Orel camp, providing they wanted it.

There were no tents to be seen, no pine trees, no campfires, no stars, and no indication whatsoever of any omelets, fluffy or otherwise, on the premises. The only sign of human habitation was a line of wet wash hanging on the front porch of one of the cabins.

A figure came plodding through the mud toward us. I rolled down the window on my side. A young man stuck his head in and said something in Russian.

"*Ya ni panimayu Paruski*," I told him.

"This young man says he is director of camp," Nila told me. She said to him, "You speak English?"

"A little," the director said, "but why should I speak English?"

"Because this lady doesn't speak Russian," Nila said. "We are Americans."

"Americans?" the director said, surprised. "Telephone message from Moscow Intourist said two Armenian ladies arriving today in rented Volga 21."

"American, not Armenian," Nila said. "Moscow Intourist is crazy, excuse my saying so."

"Must have been bad connection," the director said loyally. He was a fair-haired, blue-eyed young man with an air of quiet desperation about him. A blue enamel pin bearing a likeness of Lenin decorated his lapel. He told us that his name was Dimitri. "If you will come with me I will show you your cabin," he said. "I don't advise to drive—mud very deep."

Nila and I got out of the car and followed him to the cabin festooned with the line of wet wash.

"Each cabin has two sections," Dimitri explained. "Other side of your cabin is occupied by four French motorcyclists. Nice quiet boys."

Nila and I studied the French motorcyclists' underwear while Dimitri searched his pockets for the key. "I forgot to bring key," he said at last. "Fortunately key is not necessary." The reason key was not necessary was because someone had defected with the glass from the upper half of the door.

"See?" Dimitri said, reaching inside and turning the knob. "Makes coming in and going out much more simple."

We followed him into the cabin. He turned on the one naked overhead light bulb. "So," he said. "This is cabin." He looked at us expectantly.

The cabin was furnished with two sagging cots, one kitchen chair, and a poster on the wall depicting the

Bolshoi Ballet in the act of committing *Swan Lake*. "Visit the USSR This Summer" it said in English on the poster. "You like this cabin?" Dimitri asked.

Nila said "Ha!" in her anti-Stalin, pre-Siberian tone of voice. Dimitri's face fell. "Where is toilet?" Nila demanded.

Dimitri gestured in the general direction of Moscow and said toilet was behind cafeteria, around bend in path next to camp office, and down road behind souvenir shop.

"Souvenir shop is already closed for today," Dimitri told us, just in case we were planning to purchase some souvenirs on our way to the toilet in the rain. "Afterwards please come to my office to leave passports and wouchers," he said.

Toilet was terrible. I don't advise.

"Please to meet Nikolai Belonski," the director told us. "Belonski is my assistant." Belonski was a pudgy gentleman bundled up in an old trench coat. All four of us were gathered in the camp director's office, a one-room hut shrouded in gloom.

"Situation is this," Nila explained to Dimitri. "My friend Mrs. Kampen is very nervous, plus has a broken ankle so we must hire a driver to drive us rest of our journey."

Nila regarded me pityingly. "I will arrange everything, poor darling," she told me. "By this time tomorrow we will be singing and laughing just the way we dreamed back in Bloomingdale's, I guarantee." I managed to summon up a wan smile.

"Unfortunately to hire a driver is impossible," Dimitri told Nila. My smile vanished. "Here in Orel we have no drivers. Perhaps when you reach your next camp tomorrow at Kursk it will be possible to find a driver."

"How far to Kursk?" Nila asked him.

"Eighty kilometers, more or less," Dimitri said. "Hundred and eighty kilometers," Belonski said, and added, "at least."

"And what is the camping like in Kursk?" Nila asked Dimitri.

"About like here," Dimitri said. "Worse," Belonski said.

I dug my handkerchief out of my raincoat pocket and began to sniffle.

Nila stood up and said to Dimitri, "I must insist that you send telegram to Kursk at once advising them we arriving tomorrow and must have driver waiting." She pointed her finger at him emphatically. "Must!" she repeated. She sat down again.

"Oh, yes, certainly," Dimitri said, and he told Belonski, "Send telegram to Kursk at once."

Belonski got up and went outside. I watched him through the window. He stood in the rain for a while and then he came back into the office again. "Telegram is on way," he assured Dimitri.

Nila, who had not been watching through the window, said in approval, "Very good, Belonski!" I stared at Belonski, hollow-eyed. "Now take Polaroid of director," Nila told me.

"It's too dark in here," I said. "It won't come out."

"Doesn't matter," Nila said. "Take anyway—he will be pleased."

I took a Polaroid of Dimitri. It came out dark brown. "Autograph it for him," Nila said to me.

I got out my pen and wrote on the back of the picture "To the director of the Orel camp with best wishes from the United States of America" and gave it to Dimitri. He seemed bewildered.

"Is picture of you," Nila explained. "Brand new American camera invention—push the button, beautiful color photograph appears. A miracle!"

Nila and I dined in the camp cafeteria on something called *Biffshtek* which resembled a hamburger but had a peculiar consistency conjuring up visions of Ground Grandfather. After dinner we returned to our cabin and got ready for bed, a simple procedure owing to the fact that our pajamas were in the Volga's trunk which we had discovered was hopelessly locked, presumably forever.

"We will wear our raincoats to bed," Nila said. "In Siberia many a night I slept in overcoat and boots." She got into bed. "You want to read *Airport* tonight?" she asked me.

"No," I said. "I'm too exhausted to read."

"You positive you didn't pack any more books to bring with you?" Nila asked. "Shakespeare, maybe? *Sherlock Holmes?*"

"No, I didn't," I said. "There wasn't room. Only *Airport.*"

"Strange choice," Nila said. She opened *Airport* and began to read. I rummaged around in the emergency bag and found the vodka and the can of Arrid spray deodorant. I placed the Arrid on the floor next to my bed to spray at the French motorcyclists in case of attempted rape. I poured some vodka into the water tumbler. There was a knock on the door.

"Who is it?" I asked.

Dimitri stuck his head in. "I just want to make sure you are comfortable," he said.

45

ARE YOU CARRYING ANY GOLD OR LIVING RELATIVES?

"Come in and have a nightcap, Dimitri," I said. Dimitri came in. "Help yourself," I said. "There's only this one glass. You'll have to drink from the bottle. Cheers!"

"Cheers!" Dimitri said. He drank. "You like our Russian vodka?" he asked me.

"I don't know what I'd do without it, Dimitri," I said.

"Have more," he said, refilling my glass. "Your friend don't drink?" he inquired. "No," I said. "It will bother her if we talk?" Dimitri asked.

"Talk," Nila said, from behind *Airport*. "I am reading."

Dimitri took another drink and asked me the name of the book Nila was reading. "*Airport*," I said.

"Never heard of," Dimitri said. "Is it good book?"

"I don't know how good it is," I said. "It's nice and long."

"You like Mock Twain?" Dimitri inquired.

"Yes," I said. "Very much."

"Mock Twain is your greatest American writer," Dimitri informed me. "Also Ernest Hemingway and Jack London." He had some more vodka. "Who is your favorite Soviet author?" he asked me. Before I could answer, Nila said very loudly, from behind *Airport*, "Boris Pasternak." There was a brief but potent silence.

"Ah," Dimitri said, drinking some more vodka. "Pasternak." He shook his head sadly. "Here in Soviet Union we don't discuss Pasternak."

Nila snorted and turned a page.

"I fear that vodka is finished," Dimitri said. I told him there was another bottle in the car. He went outside and got it and refilled my glass and drank some himself. "Who else you like among our Soviet authors?" he asked me.

"Svetlana Alliluyeva," Nila said, turning a page.

"Ah," Dimitri said again. "Svetlana." He sighed. "This

46

author is daughter of Joseph Stalin," he said. "She defected from Soviet Union, did you know that?"

"Certainly we know that," Nila said. "What you think we are—idiots?"

"Nila!" I said.

"Why you say 'Nila?'" Nila inquired innocently. "What did I say? I am busy reading *Airport*. Interesting book." She went back to *Airport*. Dimitri and I went back to the vodka.

"I also like American motion pictures very much," Dimitri told me. I asked him to name his favorite American motion picture star.

"Mario Lanza," Dimitri said. I told him that Mario Lanza was dead.

"No!" Dimitri exclaimed. "You positive?" I said I was positive. "Sad news," Dimitri said, his eyes filling with tears.

"He died a long time ago, Dimitri," I said. "Cheer up. Have some more vodka." We both had some more vodka. "Mario Lanza was great singer," Dimitri told me, hiccuping.

"Do you sing, Dimitri?" I asked.

"Oh my yes!" he said. He stood up and sang a Russian song in a deep baritone. "Bravo!" I cried, when he had finished. He took a bow. I applauded.

"Is Young Pioneer Communist song," Nila said to me from behind *Airport*. "Don't clap hands."

"Very little vodka left in bottle," Dimitri said. "Here —we finish." We finished. "Now is your turn to sing American song," he said. I tried to think of some American song. "Sing!" Dimitri urged me.

"Okay," I said, and I sang " 'Here comes Peter Cottontail hopping down the bunny trail, hippity-hoppity happy

47

Easter day bringing every girl and boy baskets full of—'"

"What you singing?" Nila demanded, lowering *Airport*. "What kind of song is that to sing inside Soviet Union? Sing something patriotic! Sing 'Battle Hymn Republic!'" She sat up in bed. "'Glory, glory Hallelujah! Glory, glory Hallelujah!'"

So we sang "Battle Hymn Republic" (Dimitri picked up the words of the chorus almost at once) and then we sang "The Volga Boatman" and "Yankee Doodle" and "On, Wisconsin!" and at about three A.M. the French motorcyclists joined us and we sang "The Marseillaise" and "Mad'moiselle from Armentières" and "Auprés de Ma Blonde" and a lot of other songs.

Waking up with a hangover in the rain in Russia is about the same as waking up with a hangover in the rain in America except that in Russia the aspirin is locked in the trunk of the car.

I ran my tongue across my teeth. "Ugh," I said. I took my toothbrush and staggered out to the porch. At the same moment one of the French motorcyclists staggered out to his porch. "*Mon Dieu!*" he groaned at the sight of me. He went back inside.

I held my toothbrush under the rain and brushed my teeth, meanwhile contemplating a poster of Lenin that was nailed up next to the door. After I finished brushing my teeth I went inside and got dressed. Everything I put on was clammy. "I'm afraid I'm beginning to smell," I told Nila. She loaned me her Arpège. I doused myself with it but it didn't help much.

"Wrong wouch," Belonski told me. Nila and I were in the process of checking out of the Orel camp. So far it had taken us the better part of an hour. My passport case was bulging with brand-new very important documents testifying that we had refrained from damaging any of the Soviet Union's towels, sheets, pillowcases, washcloths, or electricity while resting (the Soviet Union's word, not ours) at the camp.

"Is this the right voucher?" I asked, giving Belonski a different one. Belonski took it, handed it to Dimitri, who stamped and signed it and then handed it back to Belonski, who locked it up in a metal safe. Dimitri returned our passports and visas after which the four of us shook hands and said good-bye, hopefully forever.

"Only two kilometers along road is beautiful new café where you ladies may stop and have hot breakfast," Belonski told us.

"Marvelous!" Nila said. She seemed so pleased at the prospect that I didn't have the heart to tell her that there was not going to be any café, either old or new, any more than there was going to be any telegram or any driver waiting for us when we got to Kursk.

"Good-bye, dear ladies," Dimitri said. He was obviously suffering from a monumental hangover. "You absolutely certain Mario Lanza is dead?" he asked me. I told him I was certain.

"Sad, sad news," he said. "Who would have believed such a thing?" He shook hands with Nila and me once more. "*S'bogem*," he said.

"What does '*S'bogem*' mean?" I asked Nila.

"Means 'God should only go with you,'" Nila said. "'Please God.'"

We drove out through the gates and immediately came to a crossroad. The sign said ←KURSK→.

I stopped the car. "What does the map say?" I asked Nila.

"Difficult to tell from map," Nila said. "Could be either way. Let's try to the right."

The rain was coming down harder than ever. "We should be arriving soon at beautiful new café," Nila said. She peered out through the windshield. "Stop—here is coming something."

"Beautiful new café?" I asked.

"No," Nila said. "Very angry Militiaman."

I stopped the car and rolled down the window. The Militiaman began shouting at me in Russian.

"Don't be nervous," Nila told me, "but Militiaman says you under arrest." My heart sank. "We having a little adventure, yes?" Nila said gaily. "Arrested—just imagine!"

"But why?" I asked. "What did I do?"

"You didn't do anything," Nila said. "Car is dirty."

"Of course it's dirty," I said. "We've been driving through mud since we left Moscow."

"Militiaman says if we wash car he will let us go with ten ruble fine," Nila said. "*Now?*" I said. "Immediate," Nila said.

"Do you mean that he expects us to get out and wash this car here and now in the rain?" I said.

"Not only expects," Nila said. "Insists."

So we got out and washed the Volga then and there in the rain.

CHAPTER FOUR

Man is a pliable animal, a being who gets accustomed to everything!

Fyodor Dostoyevsky

Outside of an occasional ominous clicking and rattling from under the hood of the Volga our drive from Orel to Kursk was uneventful.

The roadbed was perfect. This road, which runs from Moscow all the way down to the Caucasus, is wide, well paved, and in excellent repair. It is the only north-south paved highway in that part of Russia. There are secondary roads leading off from it but they are mostly dirt roads connecting the collective farms with the main highway. For long stretches we saw hardly any traffic at all. Then there would suddenly be a line of trucks carrying produce or people to and from the villages and farms. There were a great many buses and motorcycles but relatively few private cars.

In the smaller villages people stared at us in astonishment when we drove through because very few women drive automobiles in Russia. These villages had an atmos-

51

phere of poverty and despair about them that was almost physically oppressive.

Old women walked their cows on leashes along the side of the road. Other women and small children stood at the roadside like statues in sun and wind and rain holding out fruit for sale. The houses were very old and falling into ruin. The poorer the village the more statues of Lenin and Hail-to-the-Glorious-Communist-Party banners we saw.

Between the villages, particularly in the Ukraine, the landscape was green and lush. There was no litter messing up the landscape—probably, as Nila said, because there is nothing in the Soviet Union to litter with. Even the paper napkins in Russian restaurants are cut up into little triangles, thereby making half a dozen paper napkins (all of them useless) out of one.

We pulled up at the Kursk camp late in the afternoon. There was no telegram from Nikolai Belonski and there were no drivers either.

"But don't worry, poor darling," Nila said to me. "When we get to our next camp in Kharkov will be plenty of drivers."

"Why will there suddenly be plenty of drivers in Kharkov?" I inquired.

"Because by that time we will be out of republic of Russia and into Ukraine," Nila said. "Soviet Union consists of fifteen separate republics. Most of these republics can't stand each other, especially Armenia."

The director of the Kursk camp appeared and told us that we had our choice of sleeping in tents or in the wooden camp building. Nila got an excited pine tree-fluffy omelet-singing-under-the-stars gleam in her eye and went off with the director to study the tent situation.

When she came back she looked subdued. "Forget tents," she said to me briefly. "You wouldn't like."

We started to unpack the car. A young man with little enamel pictures of Lenin pinned to both his lapels and a hammer-and-sickle badge on the breast pocket of his jacket stood leaning against the doorway of the camp building observing us with interest.

"I am sure this young man is genuine authentic Communist Party member," Nila told me in an undertone. "Talk to him—should be interesting."

Up to that moment I had believed that everybody in the Soviet Union automatically belonged to the Communist Party.

"Absolutely not," Nila told me later in the privacy of our room. "Getting into Communist Party in Russia is harder than getting into Social Register in United States."

It seems that in order to join the Party a candidate first has to fulfill all sorts of requirements and read a lot of books and pamphlets with titles like *Tractor Production in Soviet Lithuania* and *The Theory of Lenin's Non-Class Ideology in Relation to Manufacturing Potentials on the Kerch Peninsula.* If he has survived these he is eligible to apply for Party membership, which is where the big catch comes in.

He must be sponsored by three people who are already Party members, and these three people are held responsible for his actions *for the rest of their lives.*

In other words, if this new Party member takes a notion one day to stand up in Red Square and shout "Hurrah for good old Svetlana Stalin!" he is not going to be the only person shipped off to you-know-where, he is going to have his three sponsoring pals right along with him. So there are relatively few Communist Party members in the vast population of the Soviet Union.

"Talk to young Communist," Nila told me again as we continued unpacking the Volga. Before I could think of a safe topic to discuss with a young Communist bristling with pictures of Lenin, the young man spied the Polaroid and said, "Here in Soviet Union we have exact identical camera. Russian scientist invented it."

Nila said, "Ha!"

"You are foreigners," the young man said. "How is it you are driving car without Intourist guide along? This is against the law."

Nila told him about how the roads were now open to foreign tourists and that it was no longer necessary to travel with an Intourist guide. He listened to her and when she had finished he said, "You are mistaken. Foreigners are not permitted to travel in Soviet Union unless Intourist guide travels with them."

There was a brief silence.

"Well, it certainly is a beautiful day," I said. I figured that with the weather as a topic we were on reasonably neutral conversational grounds. "It poured all the way between Moscow and Orel but halfway between Orel and Kursk the sun—"

"Why your American newspapers print lies all the time about the Soviet Union?" the young Communist demanded.

"What lies?" Nila asked, leaping into the fray. "Name even one lie American newspapers print about Soviet Union."

"American newspapers say Soviet Union is not free country," the young Communist answered promptly.

"Free country has free elections, citizen," Nila said.

54

"Soviet Union has free elections, citizen," the Communist said.

"Be so kind as to describe for my friend here how works free elections in Soviet Union," Nila said.

The Communist said, "Election day. Soviet citizen gets up, eats breakfast, goes to polling place, votes. Free election."

"But how he votes?" Nila said.

"What you mean, 'How he votes'?" the Communist said. "He gets ballot with candidate's name printed on it, he takes pencil and makes mark next to name, he drops ballot into ballot box."

"But suppose person doesn't wish to vote for candidate whose name is printed on ballot?" Nila said. "What then?"

"Then person stays home and doesn't vote," the Communist said. "Very simple procedure."

"Ha!" Nila said again. The Communist frowned at her.

"As I was saying," I interposed hastily, "we were halfway to Kursk when the sun—"

"What is with this 'Ha'?" the Communist said to Nila. "Why you are saying 'Ha' at me all the time?"

At this point the three of us were diverted by the sight of a procession of Young Pioneers—Russian boys and girls dressed in navy blue shorts and skirts and white blouses with red ties—marching along the road in perfect goose-step formation. Each child carried a small bunch of flowers.

"They on their way to lay fresh flowers on statue of Lenin in public square," the young Communist told us. "Every week they do this. A wonderful sight, no?"

"Only one thing bothers me, citizen," Nila said, as we watched the children march past. "This goose step they are marching. Why do Russian children walk in exact same manner as Nazi soldiers marched during war?"

"We don't call this goose step," the young Communist said. "Here in Soviet Union this march is called Glory Step."

"Ha!" Nila said again.

There were no drivers when we got to Kharkov. No Intourist drivers. There were plenty of taxicab drivers.

"What are they yelling and screaming about?" I asked Nila. We had stopped in the heart of Kharkov, one of the ten largest cities in Russia, because we were lost for a change. Kharkov is a beautiful metropolis of parks and wide boulevards but when a person has driven up and down the same boulevard and circled the same People's Park of Culture and Recreation for the seventh time it is enough already.

Nila told me to stop at the Hotel Ukraine where she rolled down her window and asked one of the taxi drivers lounging in front of the hotel directions to the Kharkov camping grounds. This is when the yelling and screaming had started.

The original driver was joined at once by half a dozen fellow drivers who surrounded our car, shouting and brandishing their fists and jumping up and down and shoving each other.

"They merely discussing best way for us to get to camp," Nila told me. "We are in Ukraine now. In Ukraine this is normal means of discussing the situation."

The first driver opened the rear door of the Volga and jumped in. "This nice gentleman offers to direct us to camp grounds personally," Nila said to me. I started the engine again but before I could drive off the rear door was nearly ripped from its hinges by a burly Ukrainian who reached in and dragged the nice gentleman out to the sidewalk, struggling and cursing. Nila and I and the Volga were now in the vortex of a medium-sized riot but nobody except the immediate participants was paying the slightest attention, not even a Militiaman standing a few feet away and observing the mayhem with a benign expression on his face.

The burly Ukrainian planted himself in the back seat, slammed the door shut, and said, "Drive!" We drove off followed by a chorus of shouts and imprecations.

"My name is Feodor Ignatich," our passenger informed us. "I speak wonderful marvelous English. I met American soldiers during the war. Americans are wonderful. Don't believe what you hear on radio that Russian people don't like Americans. Russians love Americans. I love Americans. I will take you to my home and show you my wife and my son. We will drink a glass of wine together."

Feodor lived in an apartment house on the outskirts of Kharkov. The building was old but the apartment was immaculate. It consisted of one large room with a window overlooking an inner courtyard. It was furnished with an upright piano, a round table and four straight-backed chairs, a sofa bed covered with a cretonne spread, and a smaller bed in one corner. There were several pictures on the wall—some faded family photographs and a few watercolor landscape paintings.

"I myself personally painted these pictures," Feodor told us with pride. "I wanted to be artist. Instead I became taxicab driver. My son Andrei will be artist instead of me." He cupped his hands to his mouth and bellowed, "Andrei! Come! Americans!"

A small boy in a navy-blue school uniform and a white shirt came into the room.

"Andrei is seven years," Feodor told us. "He speaks English but not as wonderful marvelous English as me. He will learn better when he gets older. Andrei has never met an American. All his life he will remember today because he met first Americans. Andrei, shake hands with two Americans."

Andrei shook hands with us shyly. "Where your mother is?" Feodor asked him. Andrei pointed toward the kitchen.

"Olga!" Feodor shouted. "Come! We have Americans!"

Andrei stood on tiptoe and whispered into his father's ear. "Still?" his father said. Andrei nodded. "Unfortunately my wife and I are not on speaking terms at present time," Feodor told us. "You have same situation sometimes in United States of America?"

"Often," I told him.

Feodor told his son to fetch a bottle of wine and some glasses. The child ran from the room. "A beautiful child," Feodor told us. "All Russian people love children. We call our children 'Flowers of the Future'—nice, no?"

Andrei returned with the wine and the glasses. Feodor poured the wine. "Even little Andrei will have wine today," he said, "because today is holiday. Today is day he met Americans in his own home." He turned toward the kitchen and shouted again, "Olga! Come! Americans!"

There was no reply. "Very difficult woman to deal with," Feodor told us. He raised his glass. "America!" he said. "You want to know how I knew you were Americans before I even heard you talking?" he asked us. "It was because you were driving car. Here in our country women don't drive cars."

He went to the window and called out, "Gavril! Come upstairs! Americans!" He turned back to us. "You will meet my friend Gavril," he said. "Gavril was prisoner of Germans during war and American army liberated him. He also loves Americans."

Gavril came in. He was a thin stooped man in overalls. "Gavril can't speak wonderful marvelous English like me," Feodor said. "Gavril, shake hands with American ladies."

Gavril shook hands with us. "Chicago?" he said to Nila.

"New York," Nila told him. "New York!" Gavril said, nodding happily. He turned to me. "Chicago?" he said.

"Connecticut," I said. He looked uncomprehending. "Chicago?" he said again.

"Tell him Chicago," Nila said. "Will make him happy."

"Chicago," I said. "Chicago!" Gavril said, beaming. "Chicago! New York!"

We had another glass of wine all around. Feodor gave us detailed instructions as to how to get to the Kharkov camp and he and Gavril accompanied us down to the car. They waved as we drove off. The last thing I heard as we rounded the corner was Feodor bellowing, "Americans! Americans!" after us, and Gavril echoing him with "Chicago! New York!"

There were no drivers when we got to Rostov-on-the-Don either.

The Rostov camp was set in a grove of pine trees but outside of that it bore absolutely no resemblance to the American Express-Bloomingdale's dream of camping in the Soviet Union. The sleeping accommodations consisted of a row of small tin windowless huts the size of dog kennels baking in the sun.

The camp director was astonished by Nila's request

for a tent. He assured her that there were no tents—was not now, never had been, never would be any tents, he said. If we wished to sleep in tents we should have brought tents with us from America.

While he and Nila were discussing the tent situation a car drove up and a Ukrainian family got out—two teen-age boys, a small girl, a mother, a father, an elderly grandmother, and two chickens. The chickens had been riding in the trunk of the car and did not look well. The teen-agers turned on the transistor radio they were carrying and the little girl began to dance the Twist to the raucous strains of "Hello, Dolly!"

"Director says if we do not wish to sleep in tin hut he will try and find room for us in camp motel," Nila said.

"I do not wish to sleep in tin hut," I said. So we camped under the stars in a motel in Rostov-on-the-Don.

Rostov was where I bought my first postcard. I went to the camp souvenir shop where they sold ball-point pens, chocolate bars, lipstick, bronze busts of Lenin, and picture postcards of Lenin's mausoleum in Moscow. I asked the girl behind the counter if she had any other postcards—a picture of the Don River, for instance.

"No rivers," she told me. "Only mausoleums." I bought a postcard of the mausoleum. "Stamp?" I asked her. "No stamps," she said. "Post office sells stamps."

I drove into Rostov and found the post office, an imposing marble edifice half a block long. I went inside to the stamp window and asked for a stamp for my postcard.

"Postcard to United States requires three stamps," the clerk told me. He gave me three postage stamps, each one double the size of the average American postage stamp.

I took the stamps and the postcard over to a marble desk and wrote, "Dear mother, here I am in Rostov-on-the-Don. The weather is beautiful but hot. So far this trip has been very interesting. Love, Irene."

I put my pen back into my purse and then I took it out again and underlined the words "very interesting." I added an exclamation point. I tried to paste the stamps to the card. The stamps had no glue on them. I took them back to the stamp clerk. "There is no glue on these stamps," I told him.

The clerk pointed to the other side of the post office and said, "Glue for stamps must be obtained at stamp-glue window."

I went over to the stamp-glue window. The stamp-glue clerk took his stamp-glue brush out of his stamp-glue pot and glued the stamps to my postcard in such a manner that my mother's name and address were completely obliterated.

"Now I won't be able to mail this postcard," I told the stamp-glue clerk.

"*Ni panimayu*," the stamp-glue clerk said, and he slammed the stamp-glue window down in my face.

I tore the postcard up and dropped it into a rubbish can. "It was just as well, I suppose," I told Nila later. "Mother would probably have been alarmed to get a picture postcard of Moscow mailed from Rostov."

"Especially with words '*very interesting*' underlined on it," Nila said.

Pyatigorsk, our next stop, was where I bought a bottle of vodka. Stolichnaya vodka sells for two dollars and fifty cents a bottle in the Soviet Union. In Connecticut the same size bottle sells for eight dollars and eighty cents, but in Connecticut a person hardly ever has to stand in line to buy it. Buying a bottle of vodka in Pyatigorsk (or in Moscow or Odessa for that matter) is even more difficult than buying a postcard and stamps in Rostov-on-the-Don.

First a person has to stand in line at the vodka counter of the Berioska for a long time. A Berioska is a shop for foreigners. When the person reaches the head of the line a salesgirl writes his name, country of origin, and price of the vodka on three pieces of paper. She gives him two of the papers.

The vodka purchaser then wanders around the Berioska until he locates the vodka-purchaser-piece-of-paper line. He stands in it for a long time. When he reaches the head of the line he gives the clerk his two pieces of paper and the money for the vodka (American dollars, be so kind).

The clerk returns to the would-be purchaser both pieces of paper, duly stamped, plus his change in Polish zlotys. The purchaser explains to the clerk that he would prefer his change in American money, be so kind. The clerk says there is not, has not been, and never will be any American change in the Berioska cash register.

The man standing next in line says, "How about moving it along, bud, I got to catch the flight to Leningrad in ten minutes." The purchaser returns to the original line and waits until he reaches the original salesgirl again. He hands her his two duly-stamped pieces of paper.

The salesgirl stamps one of them again and hands it back. This piece of paper is now a very important document and must be surrendered to Customs Control when leaving the Soviet Union, which will please God be soon.

The salesgirl produces the bottle of vodka and puts it into a flimsy shopping bag. The purchaser carries the bag out of the Berioska and—oops!

The purchaser goes back into the Berioska and stands in line at the vodka counter for a long time.

There are no drivers in Pyatigorsk. There may be a driver in Tbilisi. Maybe not.

CHAPTER FIVE

Russia, whither art thou speeding?

Nikolai Gogol

Tbilisi, pronounced Beeleesee, is the capital of the republic of Georgia. Its mineral-water springs are famous, and its name means, literally, "Boiling Water from the Ground."

"Everything is going to be marvelous when we get to Tbilisi," Nila had assured me over and over during the past ten days. Why everything was going to be marvelous when we got to Tbilisi any more than everything had been marvelous when we got to Orel, Kursk, Kharkov, Rostov, and Pyatigorsk she didn't say.

We arrived at the Tbilisi camp without incident. "I told you everything would be marvelous," Nila said as we drove through the gates. Before she had finished the sentence the director rushed out of his office and shouted at us, "No foreigners! Go away!"

I asked him where we were supposed to go away to. "Go to Tbilisi Motel," he said. "Motel is for foreigners. Camp is closed to foreigners."

We had a hard time locating the Tbilisi Motel owing

to the fact that all the road signs were now in Georgian, a language which closely resembles nothing. When we did at last locate it the motel was even unfriendlier than the camp had been.

"Absolutely not," the motel administrator told us.

"Absolutely not what?" I asked. The administrator said absolutely not, never had been, and never would be any foreign tourists accepted at the Tbilisi Motel.

"Stop bothering me," he said. "Go into city of Tbilisi and bother Intourist." And with that he slammed the door in our faces.

"Actually in our faces!" Nila said. She had just finished pouring out the whole heart-rending saga (Magic Mountain, Bloomingdale's, push-the-button, no drivers at Orel, no drivers at Kursk, etc., etc.) to Intourist. "In our faces!" she repeated, indignantly.

"I can't believe such terrible behavior," Intourist said. Intourist's name was Fyodor Eidermann. He was director of not only Tbilisi Intourist but of all Georgian Intourist operations. Very important man. "Terrible way to treat guests in our country," Mr. Eidermann said. "But don't worry, dear ladies, Eidermann will arrange everything."

He grabbed one of the four telephones on his desk and began to dial a number. Somehow as I watched him a feeling crept over me that his telephones were not connected to anything except themselves, like the toy Dial-a-Tune phones children get for Christmas. After the tenth or twelfth turn of the dial, Mr. Eidermann hung up and said, "There, you see? Everything is now arranged."

66

"What you mean 'Everything is now arranged'?" Nila wanted to know. "*What* is arranged?"

"My dear lady," said Mr. Eidermann, "be so kind as to place all your trust in Eidermann. If Eidermann tells you everything is arranged you can rest assured that everything *is* arranged." He stood up. "Leave all your worries in my hands and enjoy yourself by taking guided excursion of our historic city. Basil!"

As if by magic an Intourist guide appeared, apparently out of the coat closet.

"Here is Basil," Mr. Eidermann said. "Basil, allow me to introduce two charming ladies from city of Bloomingdale in United States of America."

"Twelfth century B.C.," Basil said, mopping his forehead with a damp handkerchief. We had left the car parked on the street below and climbed to a flat promontory on a cliff overlooking the city. It was boiling hot under the noonday sun. "Turkish invaders came through pass below," Basil said. He pointed to an aluminum-sheathed statue looming over Tbilisi from its vantage point across the river. "See that statue?" he said. "That is statue of mother of all Georgia."

We gazed at the statue of the mother of all Georgia in silence. I felt that one of us ought to say something. "Well, isn't that interesting!" I said, in what I hoped was an enthusiastic tone of voice.

"I will tell you legend of how city of Tbilisi received its name," Basil said. "King of Georgia was out hunting one day and shot a beautiful peasant. Peasant fell into spring of hot mineral water and was boiled. Dead!"

"Excuse me but word should be 'pheasant,' not 'peasant,'" Nila said. "Peasant is a person."

Basil ignored her. "King of Georgia ate this boiled peasant for lunch," Basil went on. "*Pheasant!*" Nila told him. "King said, 'My—delicious!'" Basil continued. "'Best peasant I ever ate!'"

"You using the wrong word, citizen," Nila said. "Should be *pheasant.*"

"King said, 'I will name city after this adventure with peasant,'" Basil told us, scowling at Nila. "So he named city Tbilisi. Interesting story, no?"

Nila said "Ha!" "Oh, it's terribly interesting!" I said to Basil.

"I'm glad you liked," Basil told me, pointedly ignoring Nila. "This afternoon will be even more interesting for you because we will visit museum and see oldest icon in entire world."

On our way to lunch we looked in on Mr. Eidermann. "Wonderful news!" he cried when he caught sight of us. He waved an envelope in the air. "In here I have two seats on midnight plane to Pyatigorsk reserved in names of Kampen and Magidoff!" he told us triumphantly.

"But we don't want to go to Pyatigorsk, Eidermann," Nila said. "We have already been to Pyatigorsk. We want to go to Erevan."

"Erevan?" Mr. Eidermann repeated, astonished. "But you told me Pyatigorsk."

"Never," Nila said. "Never told you Pyatigorsk."

"You came here into office," Mr. Eidermann insisted, "and sat down in front of desk and said to me, 'Eidermann, two tickets to Pyatigorsk, be so kind.'"

"We came here into office," Nila said, "and sat down in front of desk and said, 'Eidermann, we need driver to Erevan, be so kind.'"

"Driver to Erevan!" Mr. Eidermann said again, shaking his head in amazement. "Driver to Erevan," Nila told him.

"In that case," Mr. Eidermann said, "I will of course cancel airplane tickets and order driver to take you to Erevan tomorrow morning. I beg you to be here in office ready to leave at nine o'clock. Sharps!"

After lunch Basil took us to the museum to look at the icons. Basil and Nila were at each other's throats. Basil was still sulking about the King of Georgia and his boiled peasant. Nila was in the throes of a violent aversion toward anything and everything connected with the republic of Georgia (birthplace of Joseph Stalin). This aversion ranged from Eidermann to icons.

The afternoon went about like this:

BASIL: Here we see icon belonging to Archbishop Visarion. Eleventh century. Oldest icon in entire world.

NILA: What century you said?

BASIL: Eleven.

NILA: Ha!

BASIL: Why "Ha"? What means this "Ha"?

NILA: A person isn't even allowed to say "Ha" nowadays in Soviet Union? (she examines the icon)

BASIL: Why you are smiling, be so kind? You don't believe this is oldest icon in entire world?

NILA: Please, I don't wish to discuss. I am guest in your country. (she moves on to the next case) Tell us please about this icon.

BASIL: (shortly) Belonged to Catherine the Great. Gift from people of Kiev.

NILA: Very nice—for a copy.

BASIL: (indignant) What you mean—"for a copy?"

NILA: I mean that this is copy of icon people of Kiev gave
to Catherine the Great. Original icon, as we all know,
is in Hermitage Museum in Leningrad.

BASIL: (X!!!+*****!!)

"What you two ladies are doing here in my office?" Mr.
Eidermann demanded.

"What are we *doing* here?" I said. "You told us to be
packed and ready to leave for Erevan this morning. You
said you would have a driver waiting."

"Impossible," said Mr. Eidermann. "How could I
promise you driver for today? Today is Saturday."

"What difference does that make?" I asked.

Mr. Eidermann said there was an Intourist regulation
forbidding drivers to drive on Saturdays. "Not now,
never have been, never will be drivers on Saturday," he
assured us. "Come back tomorrow."

"Eidermann," Nila said, "you going to drive *me* to insane asylum soon. First you try and send us to Pyatigorsk
and now—"

"Oh, you want to go to Pyatigorsk?" Mr. Eidermann
said. "Why you didn't say so in first place? To Pyatigorsk
I can give you driver immediate."

"*Chaschapuzi*," Basil told the waiter. Nila and I had
decided to let bygones be bygones and to celebrate our
last night in the republic of Georgia by giving Basil a farewell dinner at a restaurant on the banks of the Kura
River.

"Chaschapuzi is native Georgian dish," Basil informed us. He raised his wineglass. "To Georgia!" he said.

We drank to Georgia. Basil filled our glasses again. "To United States of America!" Nila said. We all drank to that. This time it was my turn.

"To friendship!" I said, at which five men at the next table leaped to their feet and, raising their glasses, drank to friendship right along with us. It was Basil's turn again.

"*Mir!*" he said. "What's that?" I asked Nila. "Peace," she said. This toast so overwhelmed the entire company that the next thing I knew we were all at one big table and somebody had ordered more wine.

"'When the wine is strong the enemies are weak,'" Basil said. "Ancient Georgian proverb." The waiter arrived with our Chaschapuzi. In case you are ever in Georgia and feel the urge to order it, Chaschapuzi consists of melted cheese served in a patty shell of fried Firestone tire.

"Why you are not eating the Chaschapuzi?" Basil asked me.

"I can't cut it, Basil," I said. "'What the fork cannot cut the stomach cannot digest.' Ancient Connecticut proverb."

The waiter served more wine. "Take Polaroid of waiter," Nila told me. I took a Polaroid of the waiter. It caused an immediate sensation.

"To Polaroid!" Basil said. So we drank to Polaroid and to the Russian cosmonauts and the American astronauts and a girl named Tatiana Frobizher and the moon walk and Ernest Hemingway and after that I lost track.

The chambermaid came charging into my room with

the first rays of the sun, dragging her vacuum cleaner behind her. I groaned. "Please go away," I said. "I'm sick."

"*Ni panimayu,*" the chambermaid said. I pointed to my stomach and made a horrible face.

"Sick!" I said. (My Russian pantomime repertoire had by this time expanded to include hangover, engine trouble, hunger, thirst, nuclear disarmament, the moon walk, and toilet doesn't flush.)

"Ah!" the chambermaid said. She disappeared and returned with a glass of Kefir. She handed it to me. I handed it back to her and got out of bed and found *Russian in a Nutshell* in the emergency bag. I opened it to "Sickness and Accidents." "Myah-NYEH tash-NET lee-khah-RAH-deet" ("I feel nauseated and feverish") I told the chambermaid.

"*Da,*" she said, nodding. "*Panimayu.*" She handed me the glass of Kefir again. "Kefir," she said.

I took the Kefir into the bathroom and poured it down the drain, although "pour" may not be the precise word for what Kefir does when you empty it down a drain. "Bluuch" might be closer. I got dressed after that, avoiding my reflection in the mirror. I heard the telephone ring. I went into the bedroom and answered it.

"Hello?" I said. Somebody coughed. "Who is this?" I asked. There was a roar of wind at the other end of the wire. (The communications system in the Soviet Union has an eerie quality about it, as though Franz Kafka was in charge of the telephone company.) "Is anyone there?" I asked. There was a series of clicks and the phone went dead.

"Why you didn't answer the phone?" Nila said. "I called to see if you are ready for breakfast."

72

We went downstairs to the restaurant. The sign on the door said "Open 7 A.M." but when we walked in the manager blocked our way. "Dining room is closed," he told us.

"Sign on door says 'Open 7 A.M.,'" Nila said.

"Sign on door has no connection with actual situation," the manager said. "Come back later. Situation may improve."

Nila and I waited in the lobby for a while and then we tried again. The manager was no longer in sight. We sat down at a table and a waitress handed us a menu printed in Georgian and decorated with flyspecks, gravy, and other interesting memorabilia.

"What you want?" she said. I told her I wanted orange juice, poached eggs, toast and coffee. "Kitchen is closed," she said, and went away.

We sat there for about ten minutes and then we got up and left. We tried to get something to eat at the buffet off the lobby but all they had was mineral water. Tbilisi mineral water tastes so awful I was forced to the conclusion that when Basil said "peasant" he *meant* "peasant."

"I can't believe my eyes!" Mr. Eidermann said. "Why you two ladies are not in Erevan?"

"I absolutely can't stand it from this man any more," Nila told me. "You talk to him." She went over to the window and stood there, gazing out at the city.

I spoke as calmly as I could. "Mr. Eidermann," I said, "you told us to come back this morning and you would have a driver waiting to drive us to Erevan."

"Yesterday," Mr. Eidermann said.

"Today," I said. "We were here yesterday and you told us there are no Intourist drivers on Saturdays."

"*I* told you that?" Mr. Eidermann was shocked. "No, no, my dear lady, Eidermann could never tell you such a thing because truth is that Intourist has plenty of drivers on Saturday. Sunday is day that Intourist has no drivers."

"But you said Saturday!" I told him. My voice was beginning to crack. "You *did!*" I said.

"Let me absolutely double check the situation," Mr. Eidermann said, picking up one of the telephones and dialing and dialing and dialing until I thought I would scream.

"Who you calling, Eidermann?" Nila inquired. "You dialed enough already to ring up astronauts on the moon."

Mr. Eiderman placed the telephone receiver back in its cradle. He shook his head. "Too bad," he said sorrowfully.

"Too bad what?" I demanded. Mr. Eidermann said too bad we hadn't gone to Erevan yesterday when there were drivers available.

"Maybe tomorrow," he said. "If not tomorrow, Tuesday for sure."

We ended up driving ourselves to Erevan. "There is a beautiful modern road through Caucasus all the way from Tbilisi to Erevan," Mr. Eidermann assured us. "Straight, like an arrow."

Mr. Eidermann should live so long. The road from Tbilisi to Erevan is *not* straight like an arrow and in certain places, particularly in the republic of Azerbaijan, it loses all interest in being a road at all. Whatever it is, the Azerbaijanians spend a good deal of their time crouching at the side of it.

There is not much doing in Azerbaijan.

74

CHAPTER SIX

Beautiful Lake Sevan Awaits You!

Intourist Booklet

We rolled into Erevan, capital of Armenia, on a sizzling August afternoon. Anyone who is even faintly interested in where the capital of Armenia is located can find it on the map way down on the Turkish border near beautiful Lake Sevan. Erevan is as far south as it is possible to go in the Soviet Union and still be in the Soviet Union. Erevan is sometimes spelled Erivan, Yerevan, or Yerivan.

If anyone finds it impossible to get away for two weeks in August, the illusion of a visit to Erevan can be duplicated by putting on heavy winter underwear and several fur coats and locking oneself into the attic, first turning up the thermostat as high as it will go. Ninety-nine degrees fahrenheit would not be excessive.

Nila and I drove around the city ten or twelve times owing to Nila's insistence on asking directions from Militiamen who did not know where the Hotel Armenia was located but would rather die than admit it. At last Nila sat back, folded her arms, and announced, "Well, we lost."

75

Since I had considered myself lost from the moment I stepped off the Finnair plane in Moscow, this new development had no effect on me one way or another.

"I will ask one more Militiaman," Nila said. She called out through the window, "Hotel Armenia—where is?" The Militiaman pointed at the hotel, which was directly in front of us. I parked the Volga and Nila and I got out. "I advise to lock," the Militiaman told us. I locked.

We went into the hotel. The Intourist office, on the first floor, was deserted except for a depressed-looking cleaning lady mopping the floor. Nila and I sat down in front of the biggest desk and prepared to wait. Somewhere in the vicinity a radio was blaring out "Hello, Dolly!" in English.

After about twenty minutes Intourist came in and sat down behind the desk. She was a peroxide blonde in a flowered cotton dress.

"Do you speak English?" Nila asked her.

"Oh, yes, certainly," Intourist said. "What you want?"

"I am Mrs. Magidoff," Nila said, "and this is Mrs. Kampen. We have just arrived in Erevan and we must make arrangements for our camping trip at Lake Sevan— what's wrong?"

Intourist had turned white. "Who?" she demanded hoarsely. "Who you say you are?"

"Magidoff and Kampen," Nila told her.

"Magidoff?" Intourist repeated. "Kampen? You sure?"

"Certainly we're sure," Nila said. "You think we don't know who we are?"

Intourist leaned across her desk and inquired, "Tell me please, how you two ladies entered the Soviet Union?"

At this point the cleaning lady began mopping my shoes. I raised my feet off the floor.

"What you mean, how we entered the Soviet Union?" Nila said to Intourist. "We entered through Moscow Airport Customs Control, natural. You think maybe we smuggled ourselves across Turkish border rolled up in a rug?" She laughed. "Now if you will please be so kind as to give us coupons for camping at Lake—"

"Impossible," Intourist said. The cleaning lady finished mopping. I lowered my feet to the floor.

"What 'impossible?'" Nila said.

"Impossible you are here in Erevan," Intourist said. "Well, hello, Dolly! Well, hello, Dolly! It's so nice to have you back where you belong!" the man on the radio shouted. "I have telegram here from Moscow," Intourist said, "informing us you never arrived."

"Let me see this telegram," Nila said. Intourist handed it to her.

"Ha!" Nila said. "Moscow Intourist is crazy, I said so before but now I'm positive—crazy! Insane!"

"What does the telegram say?" I asked Nila.

"Telegram says," Nila told me, "'Tourists from U.S.A. Magidoff and Kampen never arrived Moscow Airport. Cancel all reservations. Signed: Bogdanova.'"

"A thousand pardons," a small Chinese man said to Intourist. "Allow me to please to introduce myself. I am Dr. Wing, member of Peking delegation to Dental Symposium. Other delegates have instructed me to register fierce complaint with Intourist office concerning conditions of assigned rooms—"

"Bogdanova is unusual name," Nila told me. "Means, literally, Gift From God." "You're looking swell, Dolly! I can tell, Dolly! You're still glowin' you're still growin' you're still goin' strong!" the man on the radio sang.

"Later," Intourist told Dr. Wing. "I am talking to these ladies at the moment."

Dr. Wing sat down in a vacant chair next to mine and said, "I will wait." The cleaning lady came over and began to mop his shoes.

"So you can see, of course," Intourist said to Nila, taking back the telegram, "why it is impossible."

"Why *what* is impossible?" Nila asked. Intourist said, "Everything." I got out my pillbox and took a tranquilizer.

"But we are here!" Nila told Intourist. "We have a car, we have vouchers, we have our passports—see?" She shoved the passports across the desk to Intourist. "Passports are stamped Moscow!" Nila said.

Intourist examined the passports with a puzzled frown. "I will telegraph Moscow for instructions," she said at last.

"And what we are supposed to do while you telegraph Moscow?" asked Nila. "We supposed to sit here and starve to death? We need coupons for food. We need coupons to go tomorrow to Lake Sevan."

"To where?" Intourist said.

"Sevan!" Nila said impatiently. "We have vouchers for two weeks fishing at Lake Sevan with guide and tent and fishing equipment."

"Impossible," Intourist said.

"Dolly please don't stay away! Dolly please don't stay away! Dolly please don't stay away so long!" the man on the radio shouted. The cleaning lady finished mopping and left. I took another tranquilizer.

"Why impossible?" asked Nila.

"Because Sevan is closed to foreign tourists," Intourist said.

"Bloomingdale's assured us positively—" Nila began,

but Intourist said, "Lake Sevan has been closed to foreign tourists for past three years."

"We traveled seven thousand miles from United States of America to fish in Lake Sevan," Nila said, "and now you tell us impossible. What we are supposed to do here in Erevan for two weeks if we can't fish, be so kind as to inform me?"

"Erevan is very historic city," Intourist said. "Here we have many interesting things to see."

"Name one," Nila said.

"You want to visit a tea factory?" Intourist asked. "No," Nila said.

"You interested in icons?" Intourist inquired. "In museum in old part of city we have many ancient icons."

"Absolutely not," Nila said. "We already saw enough icons in Tbilisi to last us rest of our lives."

"I yi yi Delilah!" the man on the radio began to sing at the top of his lungs. "I love you Delilah I want you should only be mine!" "You interested in ruins?" Intourist said to Nila.

Nila shook her head. "Ruins of oldest Armenian Orthodox cathedral in entire world," Intourist said. Nila replied firmly, "Not interested."

"I need you Delilah i yi yi i yi yi!" the man on the radio sang. "Ararat!" Intourist said to Nila. "We have here in Erevan Museum actual piece of Noah's Ark from Mount Ararat! Imagine such a marvelous thing!"

"Not interested," Nila said.

"You impossible!" Intourist cried in exasperation. "You don't want icons, you don't want ruins, you don't want tea factory, you don't want Noah's Ark! What you want from me?"

"Lake Sevan," said Nila.

"How many times I have to tell you impossible!" Intourist said. Intourist was almost shouting by this time.

"In that case I demand to see chief of bureau," Nila said. Intourist said chief was out of city arranging accommodations for world-wide symposium of dentists gathering to meet in convention at Lake Sevan.

"So!" said Nila. "Dentists are allowed to go to Lake Sevan but we aren't?" Intourist explained that the dentists were not coming to Lake Sevan either to camp or to fish.

"They coming from all over world to discuss teeth," Intourist said.

"And where they are staying while they are at Sevan?" Nila wanted to know.

"Big new hotel," Intourist said.

"Fine. We will stay at big new hotel also," Nila said. "We will fish during day and stay in hotel at night. No problem."

"Hotel is full of dentists!" Intourist said. "Are you dentist? No. Then is impossible for you to stay at Lake Sevan!"

They glared at each other. Suddenly I saw a crafty look come into Nila's eye. She leaned confidentially across the desk and said to Intourist, "Let me explain to you woman to woman exactly what situation is."

She hitched her chair closer. "My friend Mrs. Kampen," Nila said to Intourist, "happens to be extremely wealthy world-famous fisherman who already fished in every important lake in world excepting one. You know which one that is?" Intourist shook her head. "Sevan!" Nila said, and leaned back in her chair.

Intourist turned and looked at me. I gazed back at her,

trying my best to look like an extremely wealthy world-famous fisherman.

"Unhappily," Nila continued, "Mrs. Kampen is also extremely nervous person." She paused and tapped her forehead significantly. Intourist nodded. "As a matter of fact," Nila said, "Mrs. Kampen is so nervous that after we leave Erevan I am taking her to sanatorium at Tschaltubo so she can take cure."

"Oh, Tschaltubo is marvelous place!" Intourist exclaimed. She was all womanly sympathy now that she realized she was dealing with an insane world-famous fisherman. "Your friend will come out from sanatorium a new person, I guarantee."

She stood up. "Let me see what I can arrange," she said to Nila. "I will be back in a moment."

She left the office. "Now look here, Nila," I said hotly. "I frankly don't care whether or not I ever fish in Lake Sevan and I resent the idea of you intimating to that woman that I am some kind of a nut."

"Sssh!" Nila said. She glanced over at Dr. Wing. The doctor was crouched forward in his chair regarding me with his mouth half-open, clearly expecting me to have a nervous breakdown on the spot unless I was handed a fishing rod and driven directly to Lake Sevan.

The radio singer had switched back to "Hello, Dolly!" again.

"Everything is arranged," Intourist said, reappearing. "Tomorrow morning will be driver waiting here to drive you to Sevan for entire day of fishing and swimming."

"Marvelous!" Nila said. "Take Polaroid of Intourist," she told me. I took a Polaroid of Intourist, and also of Dr. Wing and of the cleaning lady and her mop. Nila made me sign them all, "With best wishes from the United States of America. Peace!"

I spent that evening packing my flight bag for a day at the beach—bathing suit, towels, extra sweater, suntan lotion, 6-12 insect repellent, and also *Russian in a Nutshell*, in the event of Nila's falling overboard while we were fishing.

At the Beach

I need a rod, line and hooks.
mn'e nuzh-NI u-D'I-l'ish'-cha, L'E-ska, i kr'uch-K'I.

There has been an accident.
Pruh-ee-zuh-SHAWL nyes-SCCHAHS-nih-y SLOO-chah-y.

He (she) is seriously wounded.
AWN syehr-YAWZ-nuh RAH-nyen.

Send for blankets and a stretcher.
VIH-zuh-vee-tyah uh-dyeh-YAH-lak nah-SEEL-kee.

At nine the next morning Nila and I walked down seven flights of marble steps to the first floor of the Hotel Armenia. (Armenian elevators only take you up, not down.)

Behind the big Intourist desk sat a skinny youth resembling a plucked chicken in sunglasses. "Where is blonde lady from yesterday?" Nila demanded. Intourist said blonde lady was at home today, resting.

"Where is our driver?" I asked. Intourist said which driver. "Driver for Mrs. Magidoff and Mrs. Kampen," Nila said.

Intourist took off his sunglasses and said must be some mistake because there was not, never had been, and never would be any drivers. He put the sunglasses on again.

"But we were promised driver to drive us to Lake Sevan today," Nila said.

"Oh, impossible," Intourist said. "Lake Sevan is closed to foreign tourists."

Somebody tapped me on the shoulder. I turned around. It was a dark young Italian in a belted trench coat—the same young man I had noticed skulking around the office yesterday waiting for his turn at the coupon lady.

"Tell me please," he said to me in an undertone, "the Turkish border is open or closed?"

Before I could answer him Intourist said loudly, "Turkish border is closed!"

"I have information Turkish border is open," the Italian said.

"You have wrong information," Intourist said. He held out his hand to Nila and said, "That will be forty dollars extra, American money be so kind."

"For what forty dollars extra?" Nila asked. Intourist said forty dollars extra for two airplane seats to Pyatigorsk.

"What about Iranian border?" the Italian asked me. "Open or closed?" "I really don't know," I said.

"We don't want to go to Pyatigorsk," Nila told Intourist. "We already been to Pyatigorsk. Why should we want to go back to Pyatigorsk?"

"I have telegram which arrived this morning," Intourist said, "directing us to reserve two seats in name of Magidoff and Kampen on midnight flight to Pyatigorsk, signed, Eidermann."

"Eidermann is crazy," Nila said.

"You don't wish to go to Pyatigorsk?" Intourist asked. "Absolutely not," Nila said.

"In that case I advise you to return to Tbilisi and discuss situation with Mr. Eidermann in person," Intourist said.

"I don't want to return to Tbilisi," Nila said, "and I don't want to discuss situation with anybody, especially Eidermann."

"You don't want to go to Pyatigorsk," Intourist said. "You don't want to go to Tbilisi. Where you want to go, may I inquire?"

"Lake Sevan," Nila said.

"Don't you worry," Nila said to me over lunch in the hotel dining room. "We will get to Lake Sevan yet."

"Yes, I'm sure we will, Nila," I said. I realized now that Nila, who had walked five hundred miles to Siberia, was determined to get us to Sevan by one means or another or die in the attempt.

She had already suggested to Intourist that if no chauffeurs were available we would travel to the lake by train, bus, taxicab, trolley car, chartered helicopter, hitchhiking, or (most alarming of all) herself driving, after I teach her how to operate the Volga 21 in the courtyard of the hotel.

"You know what I am going to do this afternoon?" she said to me. "I am going to plant myself in Intourist office until I shame them into sending us to Sevan."

"You plant yourself if you want to," I said. "I'm going to have my hair done."

"Hair looks nice," Nila said. "Why you want to have it done?"

"This isn't my hair," I said. "This is my wig."

The cleaning lady, who had been transferred to the dining room for the lunch hour, came over to our table and began mopping Nila's shoes. Somebody tapped me on the shoulder. It was the Italian in the trench coat again.

"Can you tell me please condition of Kirghizian border?" he asked. "Open or closed?"

"I don't know," I said.

"But surely you two ladies were last week in Kirghizia?" he said.

"I don't think we were," I said. "Were we in Kirghizia last week?" I asked Nila. "Never," she said. "No, we weren't," I told the Italian.

"I must have been given wrong information," he said. "I sincerely beg your pardon." He bowed and left.

"Who *is* that person?" Nila asked me.

"I think he's some sort of a spy," I said.

"He's doing terrible job of it," Nila said. She put down her empty coffee cup. "Waiter!" she said. "May we have check, please?"

The waiter looked up impatiently. "Wait a minute!" he snarled.

"How nice," Nila said. "Waiter speaks English."

CHAPTER SEVEN

> *Part my hair (in the middle) on the side and trim
> my (beard) mustache.*
>
> *Russian in a Nutshell:* Visiting the Hairdresser

I located a combination barber shop and beauty parlor
near the Hotel Armenia and walked in. The first thing
I spied was a cleaning lady pushing a mop back and
forth across the floor. It may not have been the original
Hotel Armenia cleaning lady but it was most certainly
the Hotel Armenia mop.

Before I could turn around and escape, the proprietor,
in a baggy smock and sandals, came bounding out of a
back room and greeted me with a torrent of Russian.

"Ya ni panimayu Paruski," I told him. I took *Russian
in a Nutshell* out of my purse and looked up "I wish to
have my hair done." "Za V'EY t'i-mn'e VO-la-si," I said.

"Da!" he said. He led me over to the sink. "Hold it a
minute," I told him. I reached up and removed my wig.
He stared at it, goggle-eyed.

"I yi yi!" he said in admiration. I handed it to him. He
studied it from every angle. *"Harasho!"* he said. The

cleaning lady came over to see what was going on. He showed her the wig.

"I yi yi!" the cleaning lady said. The proprietor put the wig on her head. They both giggled. I was not too crazy about this new development but I managed to say *"Harasho!"* too, without much enthusiasm.

The hairdresser bent me double over the sink and shampooed me with a mixture of Armenian Clorox and boiling water. He rinsed me off, still gasping from the effects of the shampoo, propped me upright in the chair, and whipped out a pair of scissors.

"No!" I said. *"Nyet!* No haircut!" I tried to find something in *Russian in a Nutshell* to prevent a haircut but all the phrases listed under "Visiting the Hairdresser" were positive commands—"I want a haircut." "Not too short." "Trim (the back) the front."

Had Professor Matkovsky and I ever touched on haircuts or hairdressers back in Connecticut? Not that I could remember. The closest we had come was "I do not want to sit down," which was not really very close, besides which I was already sitting down.

"Ya ni panimayu Paruski," I told the hairdresser for want of anything else to say. We seemed to have come full circle and arrived back at where we had been when I first entered his shop except that my hair was now wet and the cleaning lady was wearing my wig.

"Sprechen sie Deutsch?" the hairdresser inquired suddenly. *"Nein,"* I said. *"Parlez vous Francais?"* I asked him. *"Non,"* he said. We had now established that there were four languages in which we were unable to communicate. The hairdresser clicked his scissors open and shut in impatience. Did I want a haircut or did I not

want a haircut? I couldn't keep the man standing there all day.

"Oh, all right," I said. "Go ahead—cut it." After all, I reasoned, he might be a very good hairdresser. Just because he happened to be an Armenian didn't necessarily mean that he wasn't just as competent to cut hair as an American barber.

"*Da!*" I told him, nodding encouragingly. "Cut it."

"I see you went to the beauty parlor," Nila said to me. "Hair looks very nice."

"It's not my hair," I said. "It's my wig."

Later in the afternoon I insisted on dragging Nila along with me to the Erevan Museum to see the piece of Noah's Ark from Mount Ararat. The piece of Noah's Ark was a fragment of ancient wood, grayish in color. It could be a piece of the Ark or it could be a piece of somebody's old rowboat. Who knows?

After the museum we took a stroll through the park.

"Take Polaroid of Militiaman," Nila said. I took the camera out of its case and immediately a dozen onlookers gathered around. The Militiaman struck a pose. I snapped his picture. "Aaah!" the crowd breathed in admiration when I presented it to him.

"Now take picture of park cameraman," Nila said. She pointed to a mustachioed Armenian with an ancient Leica hanging around his neck who was scowling at us ferociously. "Cameraman will laugh when he sees picture of himself," Nila told me.

It was more likely that the cameraman would come after us with a butcher knife for taking his business away but Nila insisted. She and the cameraman had a brief conversation in Russian.

"Cameraman speaks no English," she told me, "but he says he is willing to pose."

The cameraman took a comb from his breast pocket and combed his hair and his mustache and ran a forefinger across his gold teeth to enhance their shine. Then he folded his arms across his chest and posed. I centered his head in the square and pressed the shutter.

By this time a dozen additional onlookers had joined us so while I developed the picture Nila gave them her standard Polaroid lecture—push the button, one minute, no negative, only in America—embroidering it a bit this time.

"I told them you are famous woman photographer in United States," she informed me. "You work for Polaroid Corporation and travel all over country taking pictures of bridges."

"Why bridges?" I asked.

"Sounds impressive," Nila said.

The timer rang. I pulled out the finished photograph. It wasn't bad, especially the cameraman's gold teeth, which had come out nice and glittery. I gave him the picture.

"Cameraman says," Nila told me, "that never before in his life has he seen anything so wonderful as this photograph."

"I wish George could hear him," I said.

"Cameraman says," Nila went on, "that he can hardly believe such a wonderful photograph was taken by such an elegant and beautiful woman."

"Well!" I said, gratified. Nobody back in the United States of America had referred to me right out loud in public as an elegant and beautiful woman for a long, long time, if ever. "That's pretty nice," I said. I smiled at the cameraman. Overcome with emotion, he grabbed my hand and kissed it.

"His name is Allesandro," Nila told me, "but he begs you to call him Sasha. He asked if you speak Russian and I told him you speak a little. Say something to him in Russian—will make him happy."

"Hello," I said to Sasha in Russian. "I do not want to sit down. I am an American. Good-bye."

Sasha beamed. "I have marvelous idea!" Nila said to me. "We will ask Sasha to drive us to Lake Sevan."

I began to have a faint inkling of how Joseph Stalin had felt about Nila and why he ended up shipping her off to Siberia.

"Sasha asks if you are married," Nila said.

"Why?" I said. "Does he want to marry me?"

"He is already married," Nila said. "However, he has proposition to make to you." Sasha was regarding me with an expression of naked adoration.

"What does he have in mind?" I asked. I had no intention of embarking on an illicit love affair with an Armenian cameraman but it was flattering to be asked, especially if Sasha was going to say again about how beautiful and elegant I was. "What's his proposition?" I said to Nila.

"Proposition is that he wants to buy your Polaroid camera," Nila said.

On Sunday Nila and I went to church. We had been inside a few churches in Kursk and Rostov—gloomy edifices that seemed more like museums than working churches, the official Intourist guide term for a church conducting regular services. In none of the churches we had visited had we seen more than a handful of worshipers, for the most part gnarled old women in black.

The Armenian Orthodox church in Erevan was literally jammed with worshipers of all ages at the eleven o'clock service. The building was so ancient that its façade was crumbling into ruin but there was an air of high holiday inside.

The congregation's ages ran from infants in arms through young children, teen-age boys and girls, men and women in their twenties and thirties and forties, and many old people who were kneeling to kiss the worn stones of the cathedral floor. There were also a number of sheep, goats, and wildly squawking chickens. When the service was over the sheep, goats and chickens were individually blessed by a priest in the church vestibule and then taken outside and slaughtered on the steps.

As Nila and I left the building a taxicab drew up and two men and a goat got out and entered the church. Across the roadway the owner of a freshly slaughtered chicken smeared some of the chicken's blood on an ancient runic stone and made the sign of the cross over it.

"Unbelievable, no?" Nila said to me. "Who could imagine such a pagan sight in twentieth century Soviet Union?"

We walked back to the hotel through the streets of Erevan which were gay with a Sunday carnival atmosphere. The open-air bazaar in the center of the city was crowded with customers purchasing eggplant, melons, peaches, plums, stone jugs of Armenian wine, great velvety clusters of purple grapes, huge slabs of raw fresh meat.

Every shop was open and thronged with people. The

shelves were overflowing with goods of all kinds, whereas back in Moscow there had been a noticeable paucity of consumer wares for sale in even the large department stores.

The citizens of Erevan were in holiday mood. They gossiped and laughed and shopped and haggled good-naturedly over prices and lounged at the tables of the open-air sidewalk cafés, devouring fried *pirozhki* beneath the blazing noonday sun. A *pirozhki* is a large pastry made of dough wrapped around a meat filling and then fried in deep fat.

I bought a vanilla ice-cream cone from a sidewalk vendor. Russian ice cream is absolutely delicious—full of fresh cream and butter and sugar. I ate the ice-cream cone as we strolled along.

At almost every street corner there stood a weighing machine and a line of customers waiting to be weighed for a kopeck or two. The Russian people have some sort of a national compulsion to weigh themselves in public, fully dressed and often while consuming a fried *pirozhki* or a double-dip ice-cream cone.

The people-weighing business is one of the few private enterprises permitted in the Soviet Union. Another is the florist business, usually conducted by an elderly woman standing by the roadside, surrounded by bunches of garden flowers for sale.

Just as we arrived at the hotel a pleasant-faced woman approached us and spoke to Nila. Her voice held a timid note, but when Nila answered her the woman broke into a childlike smile of delight.

"This lady saw us in park yesterday with camera," Nila told me. "She asks would we be so kind as to take photograph of her son who is home on leave from army."

"Of course," I said. I took the camera from its case. The woman's son was a tall youth of about eighteen wearing a Red Army uniform complete with red collar tabs, visored cap, and black boots.

"Tell his mother and father to pose with him," I said to Nila. At first the boy's mother hung back shyly but finally she allowed herself to be persuaded. She took her place at her son's right. The father stood at the youth's other side. The soldier put an arm around each of them and all three beamed happily into the camera. I snapped the picture.

"Soldier's father wants to pay you for picture," Nila said to me. "I told him absolutely not. I told him it will be souvenir from America."

"Good news!" Intourist said to us Monday morning. "We have driver for you at last."

"Driver to Sevan?" Nila asked.

"Driver to Tschaltubo," Intourist said. "Name of Gregor. Very dependable person."

Gregor was wearing a plastic-visored cap decorated with pictures of the capitals of the world, a flowered sports shirt and yellow sunglasses, and was easily mistakable at ten paces for a tourist from Indianapolis.

"Gregor has driven many Americans through Caucasus Mountains," Intourist informed us. Gregor nodded and grinned.

"Okay!" Gregor said. "Yeah, yeah!"

"He is careful driver?" Nila asked Intourist.

"Oh, my, yes, most careful driver we have," Intourist assured her. "Gregor is one of best drivers in Armenia." Intourist turned to Gregor and said, "I am telling these American ladies what a careful driver you are, Gregor."

ARE YOU CARRYING ANY GOLD OR LIVING RELATIVES?

"Yeah, yeah!" Gregor said.

THE MOST UNFORGETTABLE EXPERIENCE OF MY SUMMER VACATION:
A MOTOR TRIP THROUGH THE CAUCASUS MOUNTAINS

Well here we are on our way to take the cure at Tschaltubo
as Nila is so fond of saying who would have believed such a
marvelous adventure back in Bloomingdale's this man Gregor
is insane no doubt whatsoever he keeps shouting and chor-
tling like a maniac and honking his horn I wouldn't so much
mind if he honked at other cars but he honks at rocks here he
goes around another curve he's not going to make it this time
good-bye American Embassy I hope someday when they don't
hear from us we never did get to beautiful Lake Sevan it
seems such a waste to travel seven thousand by gosh we did
make it I never would have believed it if a cow can have a
nervous breakdown that cow we just passed is having one well
Gregor that was a close call and here we go around another
curve surprise! surprise! no more road nothing but a pile of
rocks hey boy oh boy Gregor pretty neat the way you skidded
around those rocks is this supposed to be the road again I guess
one could term it a road perhaps not a road as we in the United
States of America have come to think of as a road but Alexander Pushkin (1799–1837) spent much time in this part of
Russia while in exile yes Nila that is an interesting item of
historical information I don't believe I was ever before aware
that Pushkin yi! oh it is only a taxicab filled with merry
Georgians actually there is no reason why people should not
take a taxicab ride through the Caucasus if that is their
pleasure would it be allright I wonder to take another tranquilizer three today but they don't seem to be doing much
my goodness now we are hanging sideways from a cliff I don't
remember ever being inside an automobile in this position
before that's better Gregor the road has disappeared again
oh no it is being reconstructed in front of us there's a bulldozer ahead how do you say in Russian we are all going to be

95

killed in one second good-bye mother good-bye Chris so sad never to see another New England autumn by golly Gregor did it again skidded right around the bulldozer I certainly will remember the look on that bulldozer operator's face for a long time here comes a flock of geese oh boy bad luck today geese a truck is coming towards us this is the end at last Gregor GREGOR! mighty close that one a crusader's castle now isn't that interesting indeed you are right Nila a great deal of history has been made in these mountain passes I would like to have seen the crusader's castle but unfortunately Gregor is driving a bit too quickly for me to take in the sights yes he does seem to be in a hurry to deliver us to the sanatorium so we can begin our three-week cure and now at last I know what the cure is for it is for this trip.

CHAPTER EIGHT

The most important thing in illness is never to lose heart.

Nikolai Lenin

There was a doctor in a white smock, or what passes for a white smock in Soviet medical circles, behind the reception desk. "Hello please," he said.

"Hello, doctor," I said. "My name is Irene Kampen." We shook hands. "My friend Mrs. Magidoff is arranging with our driver about turning our car back to Intourist," I said. "She'll be inside shortly."

"Hello please," the doctor said. We shook hands again.

"We just arrived from Erevan," I said. The doctor said, "Hello please." I gave up and went and sat down on an old plush-sprung sofa. A cloud of dust rose from the cushions. There was a large television set in front of the sofa with a cloth draped over it like a parakeet's cage covered for the night.

The lobby of the sanatorium was mammoth and smelled of mice and mildew. An elaborate marble staircase curved upward to the second floor.

A gilt-framed oil painting dominated one wall—a full-length portrait of a dark-haired man in a frock coat, brooding over the Caucasian landscape. I recognized the man as Alexander Pushkin (1799–1837).

Nila came in. "Everything is arranged," she told me.

"Don't say that," I said. "You sound like Mr. Eidermann."

"Volga 21 will be turned back to Intourist here," Nila said. "Sad to see our little car go after all our marvelous adventures, no?"

"Not for me," I said. "You'd better go and talk to that doctor. He doesn't seem to speak English."

Nila went to the reception desk. There was a good deal of traffic in and out of the lobby now—groups of women chattering and laughing together, men in shirt sleeves and slacks, everyone seeming to be in the highest of spirits.

"Unusual situation," Nila said, returning from her conference with the doctor and sitting down next to me. Another cloud of dust arose. "This particular sanatorium building we are assigned to is reserved exclusively for Soviet mine workers and their families."

A cleaning lady appeared at the top of the staircase and began to mop the marble steps with what I instantly recognized as the Armenian national mop, no doubt forwarded to Tschaltubo by air express from Erevan.

"The only patients who are allowed to stay here are mine workers themselves or their wives or widows," Nila said. "I explained to doctor that my husband Robert is alive and well in United States teaching at New York University."

Two women crossed the lobby in front of us, arms linked. They were giggling like schoolgirls. Nila and I watched them walk by. "Absolutely fattest two women I ever saw in my whole life," Nila said. "Where was I?"

"At New York University," I said.

"Ah, yes," Nila said. "Robert is at New York University, I told doctor, and while you have no husband at the moment you once had one who was artist, not mine worker either. Doctor showed me telegram he received from Tbilisi. Telegram said 'Prepare for American widows Kampen and Magidoff arriving at sanatorium from Pyatigorsk for three-week cure.'"

"Don't tell me," I said. "Let me guess. Signed 'Eidermann.'"

"Anyway, doctor says he can only follow orders from Tbilisi so I guess we stay here," Nila said. She stood up. "He also said we can go to dining room and have high tea now if we are hungry."

As we passed the desk the doctor bowed. "Hello please," he said.

Nila nudged me. "Answer him," she said. "Will please him very much."

"Hello, doctor," I said. "In Russian," Nila said.

"Hello, doctor," I said in Russian. "I am an American. I do not want to sit down. Send for blankets and a stretcher."

The dining room was stifling but every one of the windows was closed and locked. "Patients are forbidden to sit in draft after coming from mineral baths," Nila explained. The table was covered with a plastic cloth, a swarm of flies, and a plate of black bread. The waitress appeared and set down a white china pitcher. I picked it up. It was empty.

"Waitress says there is choice of soup this evening,"

Nila told me. "Choice is either hot borscht with cold potato or cold borscht with hot potato."

"I don't want any borscht with any potato," I said. "Fried Kasha?" Nila suggested. "Boiled herring in sour cream? Pork cutlets? Nice glass of Kefir?"

I had cold borscht with a hot potato.

Nila and I shared adjoining high-ceilinged rooms whose french doors led out onto a somewhat rickety balcony. The balcony faced the sanatorium grounds—lawns, palm trees, and terraces, all surrounded by a series of ornamental fountains. The mine workers and their families were spending the hour between high tea and dinner in strolling about, chatting, or simply sitting on long wooden benches facing the setting sun.

"They certainly look happy, for mine workers," I said to Nila. "The only American mine workers I've ever seen are on strike in *Time* Magazine looking absolutely furious."

The happy mine workers and their happy wives and widows seemed to get happier and happier as the afternoon waned. There was no point in trying to nap so I descended to the lobby and undraped the television set and turned it on.

The screen lit up to reveal a large female in black lace and an unfortunate hairdo talking earnestly into the camera. She was seated underneath a portrait of Lenin.

I tried to switch to another channel but there was no other channel. Nila joined me.

"What's this woman talking about?" I asked Nila. Nila said she was giving the six o'clock Soviet news.

"She tells about situation in United States," Nila said.

"She says situation in United States is terrible. She says workers are starving and black people downtrodden. Policemen beating up students. Students setting fire to policemen. Everybody on strike. Lake Erie polluted. Fish dying. President Nixon has bad cold."

Some mine workers drifted into the lobby and joined us around the TV set. Pretty soon the news ended and the woman in black lace was replaced with a photograph of a hammer and sickle.

"Next program is not due to start for five minutes or more," Nila said. "Nothing to do but sit here and wait for it."

Nila and I and the mine workers sat there and waited in front of the photograph of the hammer and sickle. The hammer and sickle didn't do anything in particular. It didn't turn itself into a talking washing machine or a troop of Sour Stomach Devils poking at somebody's insides with a pitchfork. It just stayed on the screen.

If Mr. Newton Minow thinks American television is a vast wasteland I wish he would come over to the Soviet Union and watch a photograph of a hammer and sickle on a TV screen filling the long gaps between programs. I guarantee that before the evening is over he will be pleading like a child for Arthur Godfrey to appear on the screen with a pointer and a full-color diagram of itching burning athlete's foot.

At last the hammer and sickle faded away and all the mine workers hitched their chairs forward in eager anticipation.

"Next program is football game," Nila told me. "Russians are crazy about football. This will be contest between Soviet republics of Kazakhstan and Moldavia."

The game started. "That isn't football," I said to Nila. "It's soccer."

"In Soviet Union soccer is called football," Nila told me. Soccer, whether it is called football or hunt-the-slipper, is my least favorite game in the world so I got up and went back to my room. A circle of dancing mine workers was now stomping around below my balcony doing a Uzbek folk dance and the couple in the room directly above me were up to no good, miners or not.

12:30 A.M. (Georgian Time) The fountains have been turned off as though by a magic hand but someone has tuned his radio in to "The Baying Wolves' Hour," a choral group of trained Siberian wolves singing old Russian folk songs. It is uncanny how their howls and hoarse screams resemble so closely the sounds produced by the human voice.—*Fooled me completely* (Jack Gould, New York *Times*). *Ed Sullivan should nab this unique act for his Sunday niter!* (Abel Green, *Variety*).

1 A.M. The Russian expression for "Shut up and turn off that *!**!! radio because I'm trying to sleep" is not listed in *Russian in a Nutshell.*

1:30 A.M. Somewhere in the Soviet Union another football game is underway. From what I can decipher from the shouts of the crowd this time it is Azerbaijan vs. Turkmenia. Go, Azerbaijan! Hit 'em, Turkmenia! Rah rah rah!

Somewhere in the Soviet Union someone is eating a salami.

2 A.M. I go downstairs and sit in the lobby for a while

with Pushkin. Someone has redraped the television set for the night. Not much doing in the lobby.

2:30 A.M. Back to my room. *Airport.* Third time around.

3 A.M. Azerbaijan won! Rah!

Three weeks of this and I shall go mad. I mean this sincerely.

Dawn: First day of cure. I am led off to be weighed by a nurse. I think she is a nurse. She may be a cleaning lady. The scale is protected by an old copy of *Pravda* on which the weighee stands barefoot. I weigh 62 kilos and stand 175 centimeters high but measure only 92 centimeters around the bosom which here in Tschaltubo is the equivalent of having no bosom at all.

Dentist. Dentist's office is furnished in the Turkish mode with velvet portieres and fringed lampshades. Dentist does not insist on examining my teeth which is one hundred per cent okay by me as dentist has not shaved for several days.

Blood test. Laboratory technician is a woman, or two women stuffed into one uniform. Technician slashes my fingertip with dull razor blade, inserts a pipette, and drains off sufficient blood to transfuse a newborn baby.

Rest period. Back to my room. *Airport.* Cleaning lady appears with mop. I wait in corridor while she cleans room. Time elapsed: twenty-five minutes. Condition of room when she leaves: identical to when she arrived except for new cigarette butt floating in sink and no towels.

"Hello please," the doctor says. We shake hands. He examines the X rays Dr. Howard has sent along with me from Connecticut. Doctor prescribes two mineral water baths every day. "Doctor says by the time you leave Tschaltubo you will be new woman," Nila tells me.

First mineral water bath. Bathtub is sunk into cement floor of bathhouse. Bathtub was white marble previous to the glorious October revolution but after fifty-two years of Socialism has aged to a mottled gray. Water is lukewarm. Tub is gritty to sit in. Bath lasts one hour. Hour is long. Nights are long since you went away. My buddy. Think about something. Study ceiling of bathhouse. Peeling badly. In the company of General Rayevsky, Pushkin visited the baths of the Caucasus for the re-establishment of his health in 1820. While there he wrote *The Captive of the Caucasus*.

Bath is over. Condition of patient's hair: stringy.

Shower time. Women's shower room is located in basement of sanatorium. Dim light bulb in cage on wall. Floor slimy. Thirty-five women all taking showers at same time. No hot water.

I really must sincerely advise anyone with Communist leanings to visit Tschaltubo and take a shower with thirty-five Soviet mine workers' wives before signing anything.

Fat. FAT FAT FAT FAT FAT FAT FAT.

"What you muttering about?" Nila asked me. "Nothing," I said. "Chief doctor wishes to see us," Nila said. "We already saw him," I said sullenly. "We saw assistant chief doctor," Nila said. "This is chief."

I gaze out the window while Nila and the chief doctor converse in Russian. There is nothing to see through the window except two mine workers playing checkers under a dying palm tree. In an hour it will be time for my afternoon mineral water bath. Two mineral water baths a day for seven days a week for three weeks adds up to a total of forty-two mineral water baths. At the end of the forty-second mineral water bath I will be a new woman. Which new woman will I be, I wonder? Mrs. Richard Burton? Tricia Nixon?

"Eidermann," the chief doctor says. Out of the blue, just like that—"Eidermann."

"What about Eidermann?" I ask Nila.

"Chief doctor says Eidermann made a grave error in sending us here to mine workers' sanatorium," Nila says, "since we are not mine workers."

"Fyodor Eidermann is basically a lovable fuzzy-headed dreamer," I say. "I'm sure he meant us no harm."

"Chief doctor says he would transfer us to sanatorium for foreigners but unfortunately sanatorium for foreigners is filled with General Nasser and party of two hundred Egyptians," Nila says.

The chief doctor tells Nila something in Russian.

"Chief doctor informs me that you and I must therefore leave Tschaltubo at once," Nila says.

"Leave?" I say. "At once?"

"He has arranged soft-class railroad accommodations for us on tonight's train to Sochi," Nila says.

"Soft-class?" I repeat, stupidly.

"Soft-class is Soviet term for first-class railroad accommodations," Nila explained. "This means you and I will travel like capitalists to Sochi, which is beautiful bathing resort on shores of Black Sea."

The chief doctor stands up and holds out his hand in farewell. We shake it. He says something to Nila. Nila looks startled.

"Now what?" I ask.

"Chief doctor says that before we leave he wishes to ask us one question about America," Nila says. "Chief doctor reports that it is same question many mine workers here in sanatorium are too polite to ask us."

Nila pauses. "Well?" I urge her. "What's this question?"

Nila sighs. "Question is," she says, "how come we Americans allowed President Kennedy to be killed."

Our soft-class train compartment contained two double-decker beds and one elderly lady who appeared somewhat less than overjoyed at the arrival of two per-spiring Americans and their mountain of luggage. Due to an absence of porters at the Tschaltubo station Nila and I had been forced to haul, shove and push our baggage on board while several able-bodied Soviet males looked on with interest.

"We will store our flight bags and camera beneath the bunks," Nila said to me. "We can stack suitcases next to the window if this kind lady will move aside for one moment?" The kind lady folded her arms grimly.

"Very well, in that case we will leave suitcases in corridor," Nila said. "Hang garment bag from top bunk and put fur coat behind it."

I rolled up the Fun Fur but before I could heave it into the upper bunk it burst free from my arms (it seemed to be developing some sort of a rudimentary life of its own) and flung both paws, so to speak, across the elderly lady's lap. She uttered a shriek.

106

"I'm terribly sorry," I said to her. I retrieved the coat and tried to roll it up again. At this moment the conductor opened the compartment door to collect our tickets and immediately jumped to the conclusion that I was smuggling a pet dog from Tschaltubo to Sochi. He shouted at me in Russian.

"Conductor says it is against the law to travel with animals on Soviet railroad," Nila said to me.

"It's not an animal," I told the conductor. "It's a Fun Fur." I waggled a sleeve of the coat at him. "It's only a fake," I said. "Make-believe. Woof!"

"What in God's name you doing?" Nila said.

"I'm showing him it's a fake fur," I said. I waggled the sleeve again and said, "Bow-wow! Grrr."

The conductor backed out of the compartment.

"This lady inquires why you were barking at conductor," Nila said to me. I was trying to stuff the Fun Fur into the space next to me on the seat. It was hopeless.

"Oh,—!" I said. I bunched the coat up on my lap as best I could. The elderly lady was now regarding me with undisguised horror.

"I tried to explain to her about Fun Fur," Nila told me, "but she seems to have impression that coat is made from skin of pet dog who passed away. Dog named Bloomingdale."

"Thanks a lot for explaining to her so well, Nila," I said.

"This lady is a grandmother from Kiev," Nila replied with spirit. "If you are under impression that it is simple to explain Fun Fur from Bloomingdale's to grandmother from Kiev you very much mistaken!"

Silence settled over the compartment. The train rattled on through the night toward Sochi. I fell into a half sleep and woke abruptly when the train stopped.

"Pitsunda!" the conductor yelled. The elderly lady gathered up her belongings. I tried to help her but she grabbed the suitcase I had picked up as though I meant to keep it and left the compartment with one last glance of loathing in my direction.

Just as the train began to move again our compartment door opened and two attractive young girls came in, laughing and gasping for breath. They had obviously managed to catch the train only at the last minute. One of them was blonde and the other was dark and tiny. Both were barelegged and wearing open sandals and flowered cotton dresses whose hemlines were just above the knee.

"You are American?" the blonde asked us. "Yes," I said. She clapped her hands together in excitement. "I thought so!" she said. "You are the first Americans I ever met but I knew!"

Her English had a slight but charming Continental accent. "I knew you were American by your clothes," she said. "Your dresses." She reached over and felt the material of my dress. I was wearing a simple blue cotton knit —one of those drip-dry no-iron affairs. "Tell me please, how much such a dress costs in America?" she asked.

"It cost twenty-five dollars," I said. Her eyes widened.

"Here such a dress would cost fifty rubles at least," she said. "And not in such excellent material." She turned to the dark girl and said something to her in Russian.

"Katerina does not speak any English," she told us. "We are both students at University of Kiev. Katerina will be an engineer. I will teach English."

She told us her name was Nadia. "I hope I am not rude to ask questions," she said, "but all Russian students are so curious to learn about America you cannot imagine. At the university we read American authors but their books are very difficult to get."

We asked her which were the most popular American authors with the university students.

"Ernest Hemingway," she replied promptly. "Jack London. Mark Twain." Katerina said something. "Oh, yes," Nadia added. "Katerina reminds me that we also very much admire your Mr. Salinger."

"J.D.?" I said. "That's surprising."

"Marvelous writer," Nadia assured me. "Very very popular here in Soviet Union."

"There is so much I want to ask you about America," Nadia said. "When we return to university and tell our friends that we met Americans they will be curious about many things." She bit her lip thoughtfully for a moment.

"Two most important questions," she said at last. "First, please, tell us—why you Americans allowed President Kennedy to be shot?"

Nila and I looked at each other.

"In the United States it is the custom for our leaders to go around quite freely among the people, Nadia," I said. "They visit large cities, they shake hands with everyone, they mingle in crowds—so it's almost impossible to prevent some maniac from shooting at a President if he really wants to."

Nadia did not appear convinced but she said politely, "Yes. Thank you for explaining."

"What's the second important thing the university students will want to know?" I asked her.

"Second important thing," Nadia said, "is why you Americans allowed Jackie Kennedy to marry that fat old Greek man?"

I looked at Nila. "America is free country, Nadia," Nila said weakly. "Person is allowed to marry whoever they please."

Nadia and Katerina whispered together for a moment and then Nadia said, "Katerina wants to know please if you ladies have ever gone to Newsport Jazz Festival?"

The transition from the Kennedy family to the Newport Jazz Festival was slightly dizzying.

"I haven't," I said.

"I haven't either," Nila said, "but I have friend whose niece is married to man who rents pianos to festival management." This seemed to satisfy the girls.

"We love American jazz—all American music, for that matter," Nadia told us. "Even Katerina, although she speaks no English, can sing your American songs."

"Sing us American song," Nila said. I braced myself for "Hello, Dolly!" or "Delilah" but I was absolutely unprepared for what came.

There, in the compartment of a Soviet train speeding through the night between Tschaltubo and Moscow, those two Russian college students sang "We Shall Overcome." In English. Every verse.

"Where on earth did you learn that song?" I asked when they had finished.

Nadia shrugged. "Oh, it is very popular song with our university students," she said. "We sing it all the time at each other's homes. I don't know where we learned it. We just *know* it."

"This song has a very special meaning in the United States of America," I told Nadia.

"Yes, we know," she said. "It has very special meaning in Soviet Union also. Different, but still special. If we can sing American song about 'Someday we'll walk hand-in-hand' then who knows—perhaps someday it will come true?"

The conductor stuck his head into the compartment and called "Sukhumi! Sukhumi!"

"We get off here," Nadia said. The girls gathered their baggage. We all shook hands in farewell. "I almost forgot to tell you name of most popular American author at University of Kiev," Nadia said. "Mr. Theodore Dreiser."

They were gone. It was nearly midnight. Nila and I settled ourselves to sleep as best we could. I took one of the bottom bunks, pillowed my head on a flight bag, and pulled faithful Old Bloomingdale on top of me for a blanket. Nila switched off the light. "You are comfortable?" she asked.

"Frankly, no," I said. "This may be a soft-class compartment but the bunk is hard as a rock."

"You think this bunk is hard?" Nila said. "When I was in Siberia bunks were so hard that—"

"I don't want to hear about how it was in Siberia!" I said. Nila subsided.

"Good night," she said. "Good night," I said. I fell asleep and the next thing I knew it was dawn and the conductor was calling, "Sochi! Sochi!"

CHAPTER NINE

All animals are equal, but some animals are more equal than others.

George Orwell

In the garden outside my room in Sochi's Hotel Intourist (thirty-eight dollars per person per day, fellow workers of the world) flowers were in bloom, fountains sparkled in the sunlight, and birds were singing. Hibiscus and bougainvillaea bloomed along the garden paths. A Militiaman strolled past, whistling, plucked an hibiscus blossom from a bush and stuck it jauntily behind his ear.

The telephone rang. "Hello?" I said.

"Good morning," Nila said.

"My God!" I said. "I can actually hear you."

Nila told me to meet her at the terrace café for breakfast. "Don't forget to leave key with room-key lady," she said.

"I won't forget," I said. Russian hotels have room-key ladies on every floor and when a guest leaves his room even for a minute he must give her the room key. She puts it into a drawer. When the guest wants to get into his room again she gives it back to him. Soviet room-key

113

ladies are pleasant, as opposed to Soviet waitresses, who are usually unpleasant and often downright hostile.

We ate breakfast on the highest terrace of the Hotel Intourist overlooking the Black Sea. We had flaky croissants and fresh butter and jam and hot steaming delicious coffee in fragile china cups while the tiny sparrows of Sochi hopped from table to table in search of crumbs.

The first early bathers were descending to the *plage,* their beach bags bulging with French *bain de soleil,* American cigarettes, Finnish chocolates, Italian sunglasses, and German cameras.

"Sochi is known as the Riviera of the Soviet Union," Nila explained to me. "Very important rich Russians come here to play."

"Rich Russians?" I said, managing to beat out a sparrow by pouncing on a croissant crumb on my plate. "I thought the Soviet state owns everything. How can there be such a thing as a rich Russian?"

"A rich Russian," Nila told me, "is richest, most stuck-up person in entire world. He has whole wealth of Soviet state at his disposal. Generals, scientists, engineers— some of them are so rich they won't even talk to ordinary Russians."

She pointed toward the beach. "See that beautiful hotel at far end of the *plage?*" she asked me. "That is *dacha* for important Russians. No one else is allowed to stay there—only very important Russians and their very important families. This week, for instance, key lady on my floor told me that two Red Army generals, one member of Supreme Soviet Presidium, and Russian woman cosmonaut are staying at *dacha.*"

A white-jacketed waiter came over to our table and poured fresh coffee into our cups.

"That waiter actually smiled at us," I told Nila. A fat and furry pussycat strolled out to the terrace and began to weave in and out among the tables. "Here kitty, kitty, kitty!" I called. The cat flicked his tail at me contemptuously.

"Cat doesn't understand English," Nila said. "You must say, 'Here *kiss, kiss, kiss*' if you want him to come. *Kiss* is word for kitty in Russian."

I broke off a piece of croissant and held it out toward the cat. "Here *kiss, kiss, kiss*," I said. The cat walked languidly away.

"Must be very rich important cat," Nila said. She stood up. "Time for Intourist," she said.

"Good morning," Intourist said, smiling at us. "Welcome to beautiful Sochi." Intourist was a slender redhead with emerald green eyes. She smelled deliciously of Réplique. "We are so happy that you were able to come and visit our beautiful resort," Intourist said.

The office was flooded with sunshine. Vases of fresh mimosa were on every desk. A wandering sea breeze stirred the white organdy curtains at the windows. "Please tell me how we can make your stay with us more pleasant," Intourist said to us.

Nila told her that we needed reservations for a first-class cabin aboard a Soviet cruise ship sailing from Sochi to Odessa. "Here are our vouchers," Nila said.

Intourist took the vouchers. She didn't examine them and say, "Wrong wouch!" or "What you want from me?" or "Impossible" or "Come back tomorrow three o'clock".

"Certainly," Intourist said. "I will reserve your accommodations at once. And now I suggest that you two ladies go to the *plage* and enjoy our beautiful Sochi sun and sand and bathe in the sea and leave me to attend to all these tiresome details."

We were halfway down the long flight of marble steps leading to the *plage* when we were accosted by a tall young man in a cream-colored silk suit. Even though he was wearing enormous blue sunglasses I recognized him at once. "It's the Italian spy from Erevan," I said to Nila.

"I am prepared to offer four rubles for one American dollar," the spy, or whatever he was, said, without preamble. "Cash. What you say—yes?"

"We thought you were a spy," I told him. The young man merely smiled. "Well, what are you—some kind of a bank?" Nila demanded.

He gave a deprecating laugh.

"Don't laugh, citizen," Nila said. "If you can stand here in broad daytime and offer to exchange rubles for dollars you must be a bank."

The young man seemed to perceive dimly that he had approached the wrong customer. He backed away. "So?" Nila went on relentlessly. "You are a bank or you are not a bank? Answer already!"

The young man denied that he was a bank. "In that case you must be black market," Nila said.

The young man attempted a feeble demurrer. Nila ignored it. "And if you are black market," she continued, "you could be arrested and sent to Siberia, God forbid."

"Oh, God forbid!" the young man agreed fervently. He started to leave.

"Stop!" Nila commanded. He stopped. "You are chewing gum?" Nila asked. He admitted that he was chewing gum.

"Bad habit," Nila told him. "Bad for health, terrible for

116

teeth. Don't chew no more." He hastily swallowed his gum.

"You can leave now," Nila said, with a regal wave of her hand. The young man slunk off into the bougainvillaea. "Spy or bank, person has to be stern with such people," Nila told me.

The stretch of white beach belonging to the Hotel Intourist was bright with beach umbrellas and striped awnings which shaded the rows of chaise-longues lined up along the shore. To my surprise the Black Sea was not black at all, but pale green. A notice on the wall of the bathhouse informed the bathers in Russian, German and English that it was forbidden to wash rugs in the sea.

Nila and I found two vacant chaise-longues side by side. We stowed our beach bags underneath and settled ourselves to read. Nila had a copy of *Pravda*. I was reading *Airport*.

The sound of music and laughter and chatter in half a dozen languages surrounded us. The female bathers were dressed in brief bikinis or in more modest but stylish tight-fitting, one-piece suits. The men wore satin bathing trunks. Two young Negroes near us were deep in concentration over a chess game. These were the first Negroes we had seen since we left Moscow. They were speaking French. A group of bronzed Italians walked past on their way to the water, but within a few minutes we realized that the preponderance of tourists here on the beach at Sochi was from Germany.

Nila opened *Pravda*, read a paragraph or two, and said, "I absolutely cannot stand to read any more lies about United States in this newspaper!" She tossed *Pravda* aside.

"I absolutely cannot stand to read *Airport* any more either," I said. Nila got up and went for a swim. I closed my eyes and dozed. There was a good deal of noise going on around me. The Germans had apparently brought a carload of transistor radios along with them from the Fatherland, all tuned in full blast to rock-and-roll music.

The cabaña boys and lifeguards had their transistors tuned in full blast too. To add to the din, the Germans kept shouting back and forth to each other in hearty Teutonic voices. "Hans!" they called. "Heinrich! *Kommst du hier, ja? Bitte!*"

Nila reappeared, dripping wet. "Black Sea is marvelous," she told me. "Like swimming in bowl of warm chicken soup."

"Heinrich!" the Germans shouted to each other. "Herr Hochenleffer! Ho, Helmut! Ho! Hi! Hey!"

At lunchtime we returned to the hotel. "Ah!" Nila said, as we walked into the dining room. "This is what I call beautiful capitalistic restaurant in heart of Soviet Union."

Wide french doors were open to the ocean breeze. There were centerpieces of fresh flowers on every table, and the linen was of white damask, gleaming and fresh. The waiters wore immaculate mess jackets and knife-creased trousers. Bus boys hurried back and forth with chilled bottles of wine and crystal goblets. Each table in the room was adorned with a miniature flag of the guests' countries.

"There's the American flag!" Nila and I cried with one voice. We made a beeline for the table.

"Five places," I said. "That means there must be other Americans at the hotel. Oh, it's going to be so wonderful to talk to an American again!" It had been more than a month now since either Nila or I had heard an American voice or seen an American face outside of our own. "I feel like Lieutenant Philip Nolan in *The Man Without a Country*," I told Nila sentimentally. "I could cry just looking at this wonderful little flag."

"I have marvelous idea!" Nila said.

My heart sank.

"We will salute," Nila said. She put her hand over her heart. "We will give pledge of allegiance to most beautiful flag in the world," she said.

"Now Nila, I really don't think—" I said, but it was too late. "I pledge allegiance to United States of America and to republic for which it stands!" Nila was declaiming in ringing tones. I put my hand over my heart and recited the pledge of allegiance along with her. Every eye in the dining room was riveted on us.

"You want to sing 'Star Spangled Banner?'" Nila asked me, when we had finished the pledge of allegiance.

"Not right this minute, Nila," I said. We sat down. Before we had unfolded our napkins we were joined by three more Americans—a professorial-looking gentleman, his wife, and a long-haired youth deep in the throes of adolescent melancholia.

"I am Dr. Houseman Mucks," the gentleman said. "My wife, Millicent." Millicent Mucks had her hair tied back with an old brown shoelace, but otherwise had not done much in the way of sprucing up for luncheon. "And my son, Harlan Mucks," Dr. Mucks said.

Harlan acknowledged the introduction by a slight elevation of his left eyebrow. He sat down, grabbed a dinner roll from the breadbasket, and began to gnaw away at it.

"He's starved, poor lamb," Mrs. Mucks told us. "We've been sightseeing all morning. We visited the museum and the arboretum and the exhibition of native handicraft in the People's Hall of Handicraft. This afternoon we hope to see some native folk dancing in the People's Hall of Folk Dance and Festival."

All this information seemed to call for some comment so I said, "I didn't realize that Sochi had an arboretum."

"It really stinks, this arboretum," Harlan Mucks informed me. "It's nothing but a bunch of sickening-looking trees standing there. Big deal."

"Harlan is on vacation from Putney school," Mrs. Mucks said, "and since Doctor has his sabbatical this year I simply closed down my kiln and off we went."

"You are a doctor doctor or a dentist doctor?" Nila asked Dr. Mucks. He said he was neither. "I'm a Doctor of Philosophy," he said. "I teach." I asked him where. "The New School," he said.

Harlan, finished with the dinner roll, was unwrapping a stick of chewing gum. I felt a quiver pass through Nila. I said hastily to Mrs. Mucks, "How do you like the Soviet Union?"

"To me," Mrs. Mucks said, "the Soviet Union is the epitome of every hope and dream of civilized man since he first emerged from the cave to live among his brothers."

"You shouldn't chew gum," Nila told Harlan. Harlan's father told Nila that it was perfectly all right for the lad to chew gum.

"Dr. Michlove is of the opinion that the chewing process releases oral hostilities which might otherwise encapsulate themselves in the id," Dr. Mucks said.

"Who is this Dr. Michlove?" Nila inquired. "A dentist?"

"He's my shrink," Harlan said.

"The joy of the workers in their work," Mrs. Mucks was telling me. "The pride of the collective farmers in their collective farms. The theater! The ballet! The Russians may have their faults but we could all take a lesson from them when it comes to culture."

"We were privileged to see the Bolshoi Ballet dance *Swan Lake* in Moscow," Dr. Mucks said. "Glorious!"

"*Swan Lake* is really a stinking ballet," Harlan informed me. "I mean it literally smells up the theater in my opinion."

"Tonight we leave for Kiev," Dr. Mucks told us, "and next week, alas, back once more to the United States."

"Excuse me, but why 'alas'?" Nila wanted to know. "That isn't nice thing to say—'alas United States.' You should be ashamed."

"My dear lady," Dr. Mucks said, giving Nila a superior smile, "surely you cannot be blind to the decadence, the violence, the general moral turpitude that pervades our American democracy today?"

"United States of America is greatest country in the world," Nila said. Dr. Mucks merely laughed. Nila bristled. "You think United States is decadent?" she inquired. "Yes, unhappily I do," Dr. Mucks said.

"But Soviet Union is absolute one hundred per cent marvelous?" Nila said.

Dr. Mucks said, "Now, now, we all know that in a socialist society it is occasionally necessary to stifle for a time the voices of dissent but—"

"Stifle?" Nila said. "You mean lock up in prison and ship off to Siberia? This is what you mean by 'stifle'? Ha!"

"My dear lady," Dr. Mucks said, with infuriating calm,

121

"I really must beg you not to take this jingoistic flag-waving tone with me because—"

"Flag waving?" Nila cried. "You bet your life I am flag waving!" She grabbed the American flag and stood up and raised it over her head triumphantly. "It's greatest flag in the world and I'm not ashamed to wave it!"

She glared down at Dr. Mucks. "You want to stop me?" she said.

"That was some big fight at your table at lunch today," the waiter said to us that night at dinnertime.

"Fight?" Nila said. "Who told you fight? Was no fight. We Americans were merely discussing political situation."

It was a heavenly week. On our last afternoon in Sochi I was lolling in the bathtub dreaming about our upcoming cruise from Sochi to Odessa. There would be blue water, I knew, and pennants snapping in the breeze, gulls swooping down, an endless horizon of sea and sky, perhaps the captain's table at dinner, perhaps the captain himself, tall and immaculate in his dress uniform whisking me onto the floor to the strains of "Moscow Nights." Suddenly there was a knock on the bathroom door. Chicken Little, played by Nila Magidoff, said that Intourist wanted to see us.

"Immediate," Nila said.

Intourist had moved itself into a different office (dismal and tiny) and also turned itself into a different female (hawk-nosed and unfriendly). This new Intourist informed us, with ill-concealed glee, that there were no longer any first-class cabins available aboard our ship, the S.S. *Litva*.

"But we already paid for first-class accommodations," Nila said. She showed Intourist our vouchers. Intourist looked at them and said "Impossible."

"So what we supposed to do?" Nila inquired. "We supposed to swim across Black Sea to Odessa?"

Intourist leafed through the papers on her desk and finally said, grudgingly, that one empty cabin was still available. "Second-class," Intourist told us. "Four people to a cabin. If ship is crowded, possible a few extra people." She didn't add, "Possible also a few chickens," but it was implied.

At this point the door burst open and a man came storming in and told Intourist in an atrocious Polish accent that he was an important government official in the Warsaw Bureau of Foreign Imports (hams and electricity division) and that he was booked to sail aboard the *Litva* but that the port officials refused to accept his Polish zlotys and what kind of way is this to treat a guest in your country.

"Citizen," Nila said to him, "be so kind as to wait your turn."

The telephone rang. Intourist picked it up and began haranguing someone at the other end. It was quite dark in the office by now but nobody seemed inclined to turn on an electric light. Intourist hung up the phone and said to Nila, "You wish to book second-class cabin? Yes or no?"

The importer hammered his fist on the desk and said, "Give me wouchers immediate! Demanding!"

"Citizen," Nila said again. "Wait your turn."

"Wouchers!" the importer said to Intourist. "At once!"

"Citizen," Nila said, in ominous tones, "you making me lose my temper, I'm warning you."

"Second-class cabin or not?" Intourist asked us. "Decide already."

"Well," Nila said to me. "What do you think?"

I pondered a moment. I knew very little about Soviet cruise ships but I had my doubts as to whether their captains or even their chief pursers ever put on dress uniforms and descended to the second-class dining room in search of dancing partners.

"If we took the second-class cabin," I asked Intourist, "would that mean we'd have to eat in the second-class dining room?"

"In the Soviet Union is no first class or second class," Intourist informed me coldly. "In the Soviet Union everybody is equal."

Since we had just been discussing the distinction between first-class and second-class cabins, this unexpected tidbit of Communist ideology bewildered me. "But didn't you—" I began.

"I demand you accept zlotys at once!" the importer said to Intourist.

"Citizen!" Nila said. "Shut yourself up!" The telephone rang again. Intourist answered it.

"What nationality you are?" the importer asked Nila.

"American," Nila said, shortly.

"You have terrible accent for American, excuse my saying," the importer said.

CHAPTER TEN

Call it what you will, incentives are what get people to work harder.

Nikita S. Khrushchev

The S.S. *Litva* was scheduled to sail at midnight. Shortly after eleven P.M. an Intourist guide in a miniskirt herded us out of the hotel for a mad ride to the port in a chauffeur-driven Intourist car. We got there in plenty of time but only after several near disasters in traffic and one brief detour during which our driver attempted to run down and kill a middle-aged woman.

The *Litva*, every light ablaze, was riding at anchor with her gangplank lowered. No porters were in sight. Intourist suggested that we might find it interesting to carry our baggage on board ourselves.

"Impossible," Nila said. "Please find us porter." Intourist went off pouting, with a flounce of her miniskirt, and returned with a porter who took one look at our mountain of luggage and disappeared.

"Wait here," Nila told me. "I will get us porter in one minute, you will see."

She left. Intourist and I stood there. "You are from

United States of America?" Intourist asked me. "Yes," I said.

"Your friend is from America too?" she said. "Yes," I said again.

"Do you know Elvis Presley?" she asked. I told her I didn't know him. "Does your friend know Elvis Presley?" she asked. "I don't think so," I said.

There was a brief silence. "I know Tiny Tim," I said. "Who?" Intourist asked. "Tiny Tim," I said. "Never heard of," Intourist said.

Nila reappeared with the original porter in tow. "I promised him you would take Polaroid," she told me.

"Do you happen to know Elvis Presley?" I asked her.

"It so happens that I do," Nila said. "I met him while I was on lecture tour in California. Very nice boy but chews too much gum. I told him so. Paid absolutely no attention to my advice."

"Tell Intourist you know him," I said. Nila told Intourist about Elvis Presley while I took a Polaroid of the porter. We boarded the *Litva* on a cloud of good will.

Our cabin was down in the bottom of the ship at the end of a maze of corridors and directly opposite the public lavatory. The cabin contained four bunk beds, two portholes, and three wire hangers on a rack. I fell asleep almost as soon as I crawled into my bunk, lulled by the gentle rise and fall of the waves in the harbor and dreamed a series of technicolor dreams, courtesy of Moore McCormick Cruise Lines, peopled with sun-tanned passengers playing deck tennis and tossing confetti at friendly natives gathered along the shore.

The next morning, despite our protests that we were two Americans traveling on four second-class tickets at first-class prices we were herded by the chief purser into the second-class dining room.

"Tell him about Elvis Presley," I said to Nila. "Sit down," the chief purser ordered us. "Try Tiny Tim," I told Nila. "Don't talk," the chief purser said. "Sit."

We sat. The two other seats at the table were occupied by the Polish importer and his wife. The importer greeted us glumly.

"I sincerely hope you ladies are not hungry," he said, "because food aboard this ship is absolute terrible."

A framed portrait of Lenin hung on the wall above the importer's head. "What does the inscription on the portrait say?" I asked Nila.

"Says 'Lenin Lived, Is Living, Shall Live Forever,'" Nila said. "You want some sour cream?"

"No," I said. "I'll have soft-boiled eggs and coffee." The waiter brought my eggs. I cracked one open.

"You see?" the importer said. "Did I tell truth or not? Look how they are positively raw, those eggs. Terrible!" and he began to issue a series of commands to the dining-room staff demanding harder eggs, fresher toast, hotter water, more jam, fewer plums, and less flies. Nothing came of any of this.

After breakfast Nila and I went up on deck and found two empty steamer chairs. Steamer chairs on Soviet cruise ships are made of wood and have slatted uncomfortable backs. There are no cushions on Soviet steamer chairs. I sat down. "Ow!" I said.

While we are on the subject I am sorry to say that there are no buttons on the armrests of Soviet steamer chairs to push in order to summon the steward with blankets and hot bouillon. If there were a button it would

be no use pushing it because there are no stewards and
no blankets or hot bouillon either. (*In the Soviet Union
is no button to push.* Moscow Intourist Rent-A-Car.)

"Here comes importer again," Nila said. "Can't stand
that man." The importer sat down next to us and said,
"You mind if I ask question about United States of
America?"

"Go right ahead," Nila said. "What you want to know?"

"Why you let your students wear long hair and protest
so much?" the importer said.

"America is free country, citizen," Nila said. "Person
wants to wear long hair and protest, person is entitled."

"Poland is free country too," the importer said, "but
nobody wears hair down to elbows and yells and screams
at police like a mad."

"Excuse me but you said Poland is free country?" Nila
inquired. "Certain," the importer said. "Ha!" Nila said.
"Why 'Ha!'?" the importer asked. "Person can't say 'Ha'?"
Nila said.

"Person can say 'Ha,'" the importer said, "but this 'Ha'
I don't like. This 'Ha' sounds like you don't believe Poland
is free country."

"If Poland is such a free country," Nila said, "how come
students aren't allowed to protest?"

"Who said?" the importer demanded. "Polish students
are protesting all the time." "Where are these Polish
students protesting all the time?" Nila inquired. "In front
of American Embassy," the importer said.

It began to rain.

It poured until the ship arrived at Yalta. We had
scarcely dropped anchor in the harbor when the ship's

siren began a horrendous wailing and the loudspeakers on deck crackled into life.

"Crew is going to practice disaster drill," Nila said. "Should be interesting to watch."

The chief purser came racing down the deck past us wearing an ancient orange life jacket. "How do you know this is only a drill?" I said to Nila. "Maybe it's a real disaster."

"Can't be real disaster," Nila said. "*Litva* is in port. Real disaster can only take place on high seas."

"That's your opinion," I said. As far as I was concerned a real disaster could take place aboard the *Litva* even if she was beached on somebody's front lawn with geraniums growing out of her lifeboats. "What's the crew doing over there on the foredeck?" I asked her.

"They are practicing how they will act in real emergency," Nila said. "They uncovering the lifeboats and rehearsing how to lower life rafts." They were also pinching the cabin stewardesses and shoving each other playfully around.

"They don't seem to be taking this disaster too seriously," I said to Nila. Nila said that Russian sailors were gay, like children. The loudspeakers began to bark out a series of staccato commands.

"Captain tells crew that passengers are sinking on left side of ship," Nila translated. I watched as the crew members rushed to the left side of the ship to watch passengers sinking. "Now Captain says fire has broken out in second-class dining room," Nila said. There was a mass exodus by a mob of second-class dining-room waiters from the second-class dining room. "Captain says ship's orchestra will play music over loudspeakers to cheer up sinking passengers," Nila told me. The ship's orchestra struck up "Hello, Dolly!" over the loudspeakers.

"Take Polaroid of disaster," Nila said to me. "Will be interesting to show family back home."

It was our last night on board the *Litva*. The ship was due to dock at Odessa the following morning and according to the notice on the bulletin board all passengers were invited to attend the gala farewell dinner and dance.

The importer and his wife were already seated at the table when Nila and I entered the dining room. "My! You so beautiful!" the importer said.

I looked around to see who he was speaking to. "You!" he told me. "Why, thank you," I said. "An absolute vision," he told me. "A dream walking around."

"Thank you very much," I said.

The ship's orchestra filed into the dining room and set up shop alarmingly close to our table. All six members of the orchestra were wearing paper hats and looked condemned, except for the drummer who appeared to be simply retarded. The leader raised his baton.

"If they play 'Hello, Dolly!' I'll scream," I told Nila. They played "Delilah."

"Care to dance?" the importer asked me. I stood up. The top of the importer's head barely reached my chin. He put an arm around me and seized my right hand. We began to dance.

"I yi yi Delilah," the importer sang into my ear. "I want you Delilah I notice you were taking pictures of disaster drill with unusual camera this afternoon."

I was under the impression that he was merely singing

his own peculiar version of "Delilah" so I didn't bother to answer him. "True or false?" he said.

"True or false what?" I said. "True or false you were taking pictures with unusual camera?" he said.

"Oh, that," I said. "Yes, I suppose I was." We bumped into another couple. The importer said "Please excuse. I yi yi Delilah. Be so kind?" and stopped dancing. He was below my line of sight so it was a moment or two before I realized that I had lost my partner.

"What's the *matter* with you?" I asked him. He said again, "Be so kind." "Be so kind *what?*" I said.

"Be so kind as to take picture of me," he said.

"You mean right here and now?" I said. "Right here and now on the dance floor?"

"Why not?" he said. "Good a place as any."

"Well for one thing, I don't happen to have my camera with me," I said. The importer dismissed this with a wave of his hand.

"I don't mind to wait while you go down to cabin and bring it up," he said.

"I don't want to," I told him. "Don't want to *what?*" he said. "I don't want to go down to my cabin and bring the camera up while you wait," I said. "Maybe tomorrow before we dock at Odessa—" I was talking to empty air. The importer had turned on his heel and abandoned me on the dance floor.

Scarlet with embarrassment I made my way through the throng of dancers back to our table.

"That man is the crudest, rudest, most vulgar person I have ever had the misfortune to meet," I told Nila.

"May I have the pleasure?" the chief purser said to me. He was freshly shaven and wearing gleaming gold epaulets and his dress blues.

"Of course," I said. The chief purser put an arm around me, took my free hand, and steered me onto the dance floor. The orchestra was playing a waltz. "Take picture," the purser whispered into my ear.

"Take picture of what?" I asked.

"Of me," he said. "Who else?"

I stopped dancing. "You mean right here and now on the dance floor?" I said. "What better time?" the purser said.

"I don't have my camera with me," I told him. "It's down in my cabin."

"You could go get," the purser said. "You sure you don't mind waiting while I do?" I asked.

"Not at all," he said politely. "Be my pleasure."

I went down to the cabin and got the Polaroid and the film and the flash bulbs and brought them back to the dining room and spent the rest of the gala farewell dinner and dance taking pictures. It was a lot of work, but it was worth it. If I say so myself I was the belle of the ball.

CHAPTER ELEVEN

Hear the mellow wedding bells,
Golden bells!
What a world of happiness their harmony foretells!

Edgar Allan Poe

We disembarked from the *Litva* at Odessa and took a taxicab to the Hotel Krasny. "What you want here?" the charming registration clerk said to us in greeting. The old Intourist *deja-vu* began to creep over me.

"Two rooms," Nila said. "Reserved in name of Kampen and Magidoff." She drummed her fingers on the countertop like a woman expecting the worst. It came almost immediately.

"No rooms," the clerk said. He began to write things down in a big ledger.

"We have reservations," Nila said. "No rooms," said the clerk. "Maybe next month."

"Next month we will be home in United States and won't need rooms," Nila said. "Today we are here in Odessa."

The clerk bent closer over his ledger and continued writing. "Citizen!" Nila said loudly. "Kindly have the politeness to at least pay attention to what I am saying!"

At this point Intourist came rushing out of his office and said to Nila, "Why you making scene in hotel lobby? Upsets other guests!"

Nila took a deep breath and said, "Good! I want other guests to see how Soviet Union treats foreign tourists after inviting them to visit your country I am not talking about Russian people Russian people are marvelous from Russian people so far we got nothing but friendly smiles and warm hearts but from Intourist only heartache and headache until we ready to weep to say nothing of extra money it cost but money is least money is only money let American Express and Bloomingdale's worry about money every place we arrive so far in Soviet Union is same story go away never heard of don't make scene we traveled seven thousand miles expecting to camp and fish in beautiful Lake Sevan and what we get when we arrive we get go away never heard of in America even to a dog who travels a person would say come in sit down have a bone but no not Intourist God forbid Intourist should give a smile or a how-you-do we sailed across Black Sea in ship in terrible storm and arrive here in beautiful city of Odessa and what we get welcome hello sit down no I tell you what we get come back next month go home to United States of America and tell Mr. Nixon in White House Hotel Krasny has no rooms good-bye!"

She ran out of breath and stopped. Intourist's mouth was hanging open. I myself was impressed even though I had somewhere lost the thread of logic that led from Bloomingdale's to Lake Sevan and back to President Nixon in the White House.

Nila grasped me firmly by the elbow and said, "You

and I are going to sit here in lobby until hotel finds rooms for us if we have to sit here until Christmas." She sat down in a chair near the registration desk.

"Enough is enough!" she announced, glaring at Intourist. "I fed up to teeth with Intourist bureaucracy. This Hotel Krasny is straw that breaks camel's back."

Intourist picked up a telephone. "Just like I thought," Nila said to me. "Now we going to see a little action. Unless a person makes a big scene and stands up for his rights, Intourist despises you."

It seemed to me that Intourist despised us anyway but I refrained from saying so.

"Intourist is talking to bureau chief," Nila reported, leaning forward in her chair to hear what Intourist was saying in Russian on the telephone. "Intourist tells chief that two Americans are in lobby of Krasny making hysterical scene about hotel room," Nila told me, *sotto voce*. "If he knew I understand Russian he would be like a mad, no? Now he tells chief hotel is all filled up, no rooms left. Symposium of Soviet tractor manufacturers meeting in Odessa this week. Chief is shouting at Intourist—you can hear him? Intourist says yes, yes, yes chief—how loud chief is yelling, yi!"

Intourist hastily hung up the telephone and told us, "Room will be ready in five minutes."

"So tell me please why it was necessary to have such a commotion?" Nila said. "Why we couldn't walk in and get room like in normal hotel anyplace in world except in Soviet Union?"

Intourist said there had been a misunderstanding about our reservations. "Last week we received telegram informing us that tourists Magidoff and Kampen are flying direct to Pyatigorsk, cancel all reservations," Intourist said.

"From whom arrived this telegram?" Nila asked.

"Tbilisi Intourist," Intourist said. "Man named Fyodor Eidermann."

"Ah," Nila said. "Eidermann."

The registration clerk said our accommodations were ready. The Krasny had put us into a three-room suite (two very important tractor manufacturers had been tossed out to make way for us. I could hear their roars of rage echoing from the lobby), consisting of two bedrooms and a sitting room.

Each bedroom was furnished with two beds, a wardrobe, a writing desk, three floor lamps, and a compartmentalized sewing cabinet in case Nila or I wanted to sew something. A pair of french doors led out onto a balcony. I opened the doors and a pigeon walked in.

"I'm sorry but this room is occupied," I told the pigeon. It walked out again. "Let's do some sightseeing," I said to Nila. "I want to see the Potemkin steps."

"Cousin Masha first," Nila reminded me. "You promised your aunt to get in touch, remember?"

"I'd rather go see Potemkin steps," I said. Now that we were actually in the city of Odessa my promise to telephone Cousin Masha seemed like an impossible undertaking. First I would have to find out her telephone number, if she had a telephone, and then I would have to give the number to a telephone operator, if there was a telephone operator, which I doubted.

After that I would be forced to explain to Cousin Masha about Aunt Birdie and how I happened to be in Odessa, which meant dragging in Magic Mountain and Bloomingdale's and the whole incredibly complicated story. "I don't think I can face it," I told Nila. "I'd rather forget the whole thing."

"You promised your aunt," Nila told me. "We will ask Intourist to help us place the telephone call."

But Intourist, appealed to, said, "Impossible."

"Why impossible?" Nila said. Intourist said since we did not know Cousin Masha's telephone number it would therefore be impossible to telephone to her.

"Why we can't look her telephone number up in telephone directory?" Nila asked. Intourist said there was not, had not been, and never would be any telephone directories.

"What you call that?" Nila asked, pointing to a telephone directory on Intourist's desk. Intourist said it was a telephone directory.

"Unfortunately, this directory belongs to Intourist," Intourist told us. "This directory is forbidden for use by the public."

Nila asked if it would be possible for Intourist to look Cousin Masha's number up in the directory and give it to us. Intourist thought about this for a minute. "Possible," he said. "Come back three o'clock tomorrow afternoon."

Nila sighed. "Take Polaroid of Intourist," she said to me.

"Am I speaking to Mrs. Masha Kouzmikh?" I asked. A flood of Russian poured out of the receiver. "Ya ni panimayu Paruski," I said. Silence. I could hear heavy breathing at the other end of the wire. At last Cousin Masha inquired, guardedly, "Who asks?"

"My name is Irene Kampen," I said. "So?" Cousin Masha said. "You don't know me," I said. "Absolutely correct," Cousin Masha said.

"I'm distantly related to Mrs. Irving Pinman," I went on. "Never heard of," Cousin Masha said. "Birdie Pinman," I said.

"Birdie *Pinman?*" Cousin Masha repeated.

"That's right," I said. "Vaclav Pinman's niece. His oldest sister's grandchild."

Cousin Masha said, "Never heard of" again, and hung up.

I wanted to drop the whole thing then and there. "Let's go see the Potemkin steps," I said to Nila. She refused even to entertain the idea of defeat.

"Try to telephone again," she told me. I tried again. This time I got as far as Vaclav Pinman before Cousin Masha hung up on me.

"Try once more," said Miss Siberia of 1933. I tried once more.

"Cousin Masha, this is Irene Kampen from America," I said. "—Don't hang up!" I tried a different approach this time. "Vaclav Pinman was Novikov Pinman's oldest son," I told Cousin Masha.

"Novikov Pinman?" Cousin Masha said. "How could you know Novikov Pinman? He escaped from Russia to United States years ago."

"That's right," I said. ("I think I'm beginning to get through to her," I told Nila.) "Birdie Pinman asked me to telephone you and say hello," I said.

"Let me be absolutely certain I understand this," Cousin Masha said. "You say you live in United States of America?"

"Yes," I said.

"You came over here to visit Soviet Union?" she asked. "That's right," I said. "Of your own free will?" she asked. "Of course," I said.

138

"You must be crazy," Cousin Masha said.

I glanced at Intourist. "What does Cousin Masha say?" Nila asked. "She says she's surprised to hear from me," I said. "She still speaks awfully good English."

"Strange you should telephone me today," Cousin Masha said. "You know what I am sitting here and doing?"

"No, I don't, Cousin Masha," I said. "What are you doing?"

"Crying," Cousin Masha said. "Sobbing like a baby."

I heard an irritable male voice say something to Cousin Masha. "My son informs me I shouldn't cry," Cousin Masha said. "My son informs me this should be happiest day of my life."

The other voice spoke again.

"I'm *asking* her!" Cousin Masha said. "My son, Yaroslav, invites you to a wedding," she told me.

"Whose wedding?" I asked.

Cousin Masha gave a heart-rending sigh. "My only son, Yaroslav Kouzmikh," she told me, "gets married today to a certain person name of Natasha Afanassieva, God forbid."

"Mama!" the voice said furiously.

"When you get home to America," Cousin Masha said, "tell Birdie Pinman 'Birdie, in Odessa I went to a wedding where the mother had a heavy heart, believe me.'"

"MAMA!" the voice shouted.

"So come to the wedding," Cousin Masha said to me. "Three o'clock. The Odessa Wedding Palace."

Every large Russian city has a wedding palace where a girl can get married amid the romantic trappings of flowers, wedding veils, Lohengrin, and champagne. The cost is one ruble sixty kopecks per ceremony. Veils, champagne, flowers, photographers and Lohengrin are extra.

The main hall of the Odessa Wedding Palace had tile walls inlaid with a hammer and sickle mosaic. The inevitable portrait of Lenin dominated one end of the hall. The other was banked with dead philodendron plants in clay pots. A wooden table stood beneath Lenin's portrait.

The Bride's Room led into the hall. The brides-to-be and their attendants often have a long wait in this room because on some afternoons as many as fifty ceremonies are scheduled. On the day of the Kouzmikh-Afanassieva nuptials, thirty-eight ceremonies were booked.

When I got there an orchestra was tuning up. Cousin Masha, dressed in black, pounced on me. "Just arrived myself," she said, fanning her ample bosom with a handkerchief. "No taxicabs. Had to run through streets like a crazy woman to my own son's wedding."

The orchestra finished tuning up and began to play. "What they are playing?" Cousin Masha asked. "Never heard such terrible music."

"An American song," I said. "It's called 'Hello, Dolly!'"

"Better it should be called 'Good-bye Yaroslav,'" Cousin Masha said bitterly. The loudspeaker boomed into life. "Afanessieva—Kouzmikh!" someone announced.

The orchestra abandoned "Hello, Dolly!" and switched to the Wedding March from Lohengrin, played in jazz time. Three middle-aged women marched into the hall single file and lined up behind the wooden table.

"Fat one in pink dress is Judge," Cousin Masha told me, without bothering to lower her voice. "Ugly one with red

140

sash across bosom is Communist Party deputy. Third one with interesting skin condition is ring bearer."

Two young men with white carnations in the lapels of their dark suits stood facing the women on the opposite side of the table.

"Dark handsome one is my son, Yaroslav," Cousin Masha told me. "Best man is bum from sickle factory."

The door of the Bride's Room opened and the bride herself approached the table, accompanied by her maid of honor. Both girls wore white street-length dresses and carried white roses. The bride's veil was thrown back. She was a snub-nosed blonde with kohl-rimmed eyes. She rolled the eyes hungrily at her husband-to-be as she stood next to him at the table.

"Look how she is looking at my son!" Cousin Masha said. "A snake looking at a rabbit!"

Yaroslav shot a furious glance at his mother. "A hawk looking at a dove," Cousin Masha told me. Several people in our vicinity were frowning at us. Cousin Masha paid them absolutely no attention.

"Judge is reading marriage ceremony out loud," Cousin Masha explained to me. "Judge could use new corset. Also brassiere wouldn't hurt. Now Communist Party deputy makes speech to bride and groom about their duty as Soviet citizens. This deputy is ugliest woman in Odessa, I guarantee."

It was the deputy's turn to glare in Cousin Masha's direction.

"She tells bride and groom Lenin expects every new married couple to start Soviet family immediate," Cousin Masha told me. "Lenin should only mind his own business and stay in mausoleum where he belongs."

"Citizen!" someone near us said. "Ssssh!"

"Sssh yourself," Cousin Masha said. The ring bearer handed the bride and groom two gold wedding bands. Natasha and Yaroslav exchanged rings.

"They married!" Cousin Masha said, with a strangled sob· The deputy and the judge shook hands with the members of the bridal party. "My only son!" Cousin Masha said. "A black day!"

The bride and groom kissed each other. The orchestra struck up a tune which I recognized from hearing it played aboard the *Litva*. It was "All Honor to Lenin Our Glorious Hero."

"Enough already with Lenin!" Cousin Masha cried, dissolving into tears.

"But everything turned out just fine," I told Nila afterward. "There was a big reception with a wedding cake and champagne and Cousin Masha cheered up quite a bit after two glasses of the stuff. I'm almost afraid to tell you where the bride and groom went on their honeymoon."

"Beautiful Lake Sevan?" Nila said.

"Better than that," I said. "Beautiful Siberia."

We were scheduled to fly from Odessa to Moscow via Aeroflot, the Soviet airline, at noon. We packed and went downstairs to the hotel dining room for a late breakfast.

A pilot, or someone dressed up to resemble a pilot, appeared in the doorway just as we sat down at our table and stood gazing around the dining room, glassy-eyed. One of the waitresses spotted him.

"Sergei!" she said. She took him by the arm and led him to a table. He walked with extreme caution as though any untoward motion might dislodge his head from the rest of his body. I recognized the symptoms of an acute Stolichnaya vodka hangover.

"Do you suppose he's really a pilot?" I asked Nila in an undertone. "Wearing a pilot's uniform," Nila said.

Sergei sat slumped in his chair staring into space until the waitress returned with his breakfast, which consisted of cheese blintzes and a large glass of tomato juice.

"You don't suppose he's a pilot for Aeroflot, do you?" I said to Nila.

"Must be," Nila said. "Unfortunately or not, Aeroflot is only airline in Soviet Union."

We checked out of the Hotel Krasny simultaneously with the arrival of a chartered bus carrying a delegation of tractor manufacturers from East Germany. As we left the lobby I could hear Intourist shouting at them, "No rooms! No rooms!" in German.

We took a taxicab to the Odessa Airport and were led out to the field by an Intourist airport guide.

"What's that?" I asked, pointing at the runway.

Intourist said it was our airplane. "An Ilyushin 18," Intourist said. "Safest plane in the air." I studied the safest plane in the air through narrowed eyes. "A magnificent machine," Intourist said.

The pilot climbed down from the cockpit of the safest plane in the air, circled it suspiciously, and aimed a savage kick at its left tire. I recognized the pilot. It was Sergei.

Nila and I had window seats, one behind the other. Mine was in the first row and afforded me an unobstructed view of the cockpit. Sergei was in the pilot's seat. The copilot, seated next to him, appeared to be about fourteen years old. I turned around and said to Nila, "I wish I hadn't read *Airport* so much."

"Me too," Nila said. "If we should ever visit the Soviet Union again kindly bring Shakespeare or Bible instead."

The cabin was filled. A rock-and-roll group, complete with bass fiddle and electric guitars, occupied most of the rear section. The Italian spy was across the aisle from us. "Still chewing gum," Nila said in disapproval.

Just as the stewardess was closing the cabin door a passenger came rushing down the aisle and sank breathlessly into the empty seat next to me. He was carrying a leather briefcase under one arm and a pet owl in a cage.

I moved as far as I could from him in my seat. After nearly two months in the Soviet Union I was still baffled by this Russian penchant for taking the family poultry along on pleasure trips.

The wings of the Ilyushin began to vibrate. There was a violent shudder of the fuselage, a roar of engines, and we were airborne.

"Yi!" my seatmate gasped, mopping his forehead. "Who?" the owl said, staring out at me through the bars of the cage. I said, *"Ya ni panimayu Paruski."*

The stewardess appeared with an armful of plastic bags and said something to me in Russian.

"Stewardess inquires whether you plan to be sick on this flight," my seatmate translated for me.

"Sick?" I said. "Why?" "Who," said the owl.

"If you plan to be sick she will supply you now with plastic sick bag," my seatmate said.

"I don't know yet whether I'm going to be sick or not," I said.

"Better to say yes and take bag," my seatmate said.

"Otherwise will be too late." I took a sick bag from the stewardess. The plane lurched violently. I looked out the window. We seemed to be flying just above the level of the treetops.

"Low!" I said. The Ilyushin hit an air pocket and lurched again, throwing me against the arm of my seatmate. "Sorry," I said.

I noticed the spy looking around frantically for the stewardess with the sick bags but it was too late. We hit another air pocket. The owl's cage bounced into the air and landed in my lap. "Oy," I said. "Yi!" said my seatmate. "Who," said the owl.

CHAPTER TWELVE

An iron curtain has descended across the continent.

Winston Churchill

We were back in Moscow. Our room in the Hotel Russia (five thousand rooms, no sink stoppers) overlooked St. Basil's Cathedral and its fairytale domes. Just beyond was the Kremlin wall and the mausoleum.

The room was furnished with modern Finnish furniture—upholstered swivel chairs, built-in cabinets, and modernistic lamps. The floor was carpeted and the wall overlooking Red Square consisted of one sheet of plate glass.

"I have marvelous idea," Nila said. "We will visit Hotel Metropole and surprise Vladimir and Boris. When they see us they will be like two mads."

But when Vladimir and Boris saw us they were more like two frantics, or like one frantic and one crazy.

"My God, where you been?" Vladimir cried. "Where is car?" Boris was trembling violently. "What you did with Volga 21?" Vladimir demanded.

"We did what we supposed to do," Nila said. "We gave it back to Intourist."

"But where?" Vladimir asked.

"In Tschaltubo," Nila said, "where we were supposed to give it back."

"Tschaltubo?" Vladimir repeated. "You positive?"

"Give me very important document we got from Tschaltubo Intourist," Nila said to me. I got the document out of my passport case and gave it to her. "Here," Nila said, plunking it down in front of Vladimir. "Receipt for Volga 21, license number 5514, signed Mestronsky, Intourist office, Tschaltubo."

Vladimir picked up the document and read it with a dazed expression. "I can't believe," he said. "Tschaltubo! Imagine."

He opened a desk drawer and took out a sheaf of telegrams. "Moscow Intourist has been searching entire Soviet Union by telegram for Kampen and Magidoff and Volga 21," he told us.

"Why they didn't search in Tschaltubo?" Nila asked.

Vladimir took a telegram from the top of the pile and handed it to Nila. Nila read it aloud:

"'Tourists Kampen and Magidoff departing here via Aeroflot for Pyatigorsk. Cancel all further reservations on itinerary including Tschaltubo sanatorium. Signed: Eidermann, Tbilisi Intourist.'"

"Naturally we sent wire immediately to Eidermann asking where is car," Vladimir told us. "Eidermann wired back that you took car with you to Pyatigorsk."

"On the airplane?" I said.

"Eidermann is crazy," Nila said earnestly to Vladimir. "Believe me, citizen, you got an insane person in charge of Tbilisi Intourist office."

"I think I'll go see the mausoleum," I said to Nila. We

were back in our room at the Hotel Russia. "I feel that I should take a look at old you-know-who before leaving the Soviet Union."

"Waste of time," Nila told me. "Nothing to see." The telephone rang. Nila answered it. "It's for you," she said.

"Well, talk about a small world," I said, after I had hung up. "That was Stanley Van Appelbaum. I haven't seen him for ages. He works for the New York *Times* Moscow bureau."

"How he knew you were in Moscow?" Nila asked.

"I suppose he saw our names on file at the American Embassy," I said. "Stanley always knows all about everything."

Stanley had invited me to the Bolshoi Ballet that evening so I put on my silver dress and my Fun Fur coat and what was left of Nila's Arpège and took a taxicab to his apartment. "Hope you don't mind picking me up," he said over the phone. "I'll be working until the last minute filing a dispatch on the Chinese situation."

I knocked on the door of the apartment. Stanley opened it. "Hey!" he said. "Hello there!"

"Hello, Stanley," I said. Since we had last seen each other back in Connecticut, Stanley had acquired long sideburns, a beard, and a large apricot-colored French poodle. This poodle took one look at me in my Fun Fur and fell madly in love.

"Down, boy!" Stanley said. "Well, well, Irene, it certainly is great to see you—I said, down, boy. Pierre! Down!"

"It's great to see you too, Stanley," I said. Stanley and I and the poodle shook hands. "Down, Pierre," Stanley

149

said. "I don't know what's gotten into him—down, sir! *Down!*"

"This is a lovely apartment, Stanley," I said. "I didn't realize that you—down, boy."

"His name is Pierre," Stanley said. "Down, Pierre," I said. "Would you like a drink before we leave?" Stanley asked me. "That would be nice," I said.

"Take that armchair over there," Stanley said. "Scotch okay?"

"Scotch is fine," I said. Pierre and I sat down in the armchair. "Get *off!*" I said.

Stanley handed me my drink. "Cheers," he said. "Here's to more happy reunions." We drank. "Well, Irene, what's your opinion of the Soviet Union now that you've spent a couple of months over here?"

"Well, Stanley," I said, "I think that the Soviet Union—"

"*Pierre!*" Stanley said.

"Maybe if you locked him in another room?" I suggested. Stanley said there was no other room.

"It's a one-room apartment," Stanley said. "Oh," I said. "Well, as I was telling you, I think that the Soviet Union is absolutely—"

"Now God damn it, Pierre, that's enough!" Stanley shouted. "I'm terribly sorry," he said to me. "You were saying?"

"I was saying about the Soviet Union," I said. "—Pierre! Stop that! This minute!"

"I think perhaps we'd better leave for the theater," Stanley said. "I told you, didn't I, that I have tickets for the ballet?"

"Marvelous!" I said. "*Swan Lake?*"

"*Swan Lake* is for tourists," Stanley said.

"I'll check our coats," Stanley said. "It's a regulation in all Russian theaters—no coats allowed." He helped me off with the Fun Fur. "And a damned good regulation too," he said.

We had box seats. "Best in the house," Stanley said. "They cost only two-fifty each. Fantastic. The Russians may have their faults but we could all take a lesson from them when it comes to culture. They're dancing *Queen of Spades* tonight. You know the story, of course?"

"Of course," I said. (This was a big fat lie.)

"Pushkin," Stanley said. I turned around.

"Where?" I said.

"I mean Pushkin wrote the story of *Queen of Spades*," Stanley said. He looked at me rather strangely. "Pushkin is dead," he said.

"Well, I know *that*," I said. I gave a light laugh. "Heavens, Stanley!" I said.

The curtain went up.

There are three entr'actes during *Queen of Spades*.

"Good God!" I said, when the curtain descended for the first one. On all sides of us the members of the audience were stampeding toward the lobby. "What is it —a fire?" I asked Stanley.

Stanley said of course not, it was merely people heading for the buffet to load up on salami sandwiches and beer.

"The performances in the Russian theater begin so early in the evening that most people have no time to eat dinner first," Stanley said. "The doors of all Russian theaters are locked as soon as the curtain goes up. Nobody can get in after a performance has started. On the other hand I suppose nobody can get out either but nothing on this earth is perfect. That's an attractive dress you're wearing. If you'll look about you, you will notice that Soviet women do not dress elaborately to attend the theater."

I looked about me. "You can say that again," I said.

"The Chinese situation is fraught with imponderables," Stanley said. "Harrison Salisbury is sadly misguided in his estimate of the potential of nuclear disarmament. The rattling sound you complain of in the Volga 21 is most probably a faulty cylinder head. Alexander Pushkin was killed while fighting a duel. It seems to me impossible for anyone to fall down and break an ankle on Magic Mountain if they are skiing in proper control. Would you care for a salami sandwich?"

"No thank you," I said.

"I hope you're not planning to waste your last day in Moscow tomorrow in visiting the mausoleum," Stanley said. "The Russian people often have to stand in line for as long as eight hours to get in. Foreigners are allowed to enter almost immediately but in my opinion it's still a waste of time. A woman named Dora Kaplan shot at Lenin in the year nineteen-eighteen. She missed. Lenin's real name was Vladimir Ilich Ulanov. They've got him in there in a glass casket. Looks alive but he's not. I'll take you sightseeing tomorrow afternoon and show you something a great deal more worthwhile than the mausoleum, all right?"

"All right," I said. "Only don't bring Pierre."

The next morning—our last in the Soviet Union—Nila and I went to Intourist to pick up our airline tickets to New York. Our Aeroflot Moscow-New York reservations had been confirmed, our vouchers were in order, our

152

tickets had been prepaid by American Express via Bloomingdale's to Intourist, and there remained only the
technicality of Intourist actually handing over to us the
tickets themselves.

"And if anyone says impossible," I told Nila, "I'm going
to scream."

"Impossible," Intourist said. "I can't stand it," I said.
"Why impossible?" Nila asked. Intourist said impossible
because all Aeroflot flights to New York were sold out.
No seats. Long waiting list. "Maybe next week," Intourist said.

"But we have confirmed reservations!" I said. I showed
Intourist our confirmed reservations. She looked at them
for a while and then she said, "Come back tomorrow."

"I really will scream," I said.

"We supposed to be in New York tomorrow, citizen,"
Nila said to Intourist. Intourist shrugged. "Impossible,"
she said.

"In that case we go right to the top," Nila said. "Tell me
please name of man in charge of entire Moscow Intourist bureau."

Intourist said man in charge of Moscow Intourist bureau was a woman. "Name of Bogdanova," Intourist said.

"Aha!" Nila said. "Situation now becomes clearer."

"We demand to see this Madame Bogdanova in person," I told Intourist.

Intourist said impossible. "Madame Bogdanova is in
hospital resting from nervous disorder," she said.

"Well, must be somebody in charge while she is resting,"
Nila said. Intourist admitted that temporary acting com-
missar was in charge.

"Very busy man," she said. "Doesn't care to be disturbed
under any circumstance."

"Busy or not, we demand to see," Nila said firmly.

"Very well," Intourist said. "Come back tomorrow. Three o'clock."

"Now!" Nila said. "Not tomorrow, not next week, not ten years from tomorrow. Now!"

Intourist shrugged. "If you insist," she said. She stood. "Come with me," she told us.

"My dear ladies!" Mr. Eidermann exclaimed. He shook hands with us, beaming. "How you enjoyed Pyatigorsk?"

"No space on Aeroflot?" Mr. Eidermann said, after we had outlined to him our plight. "I can hardly believe such a thing. But don't worry—Eidermann will arrange everything." He picked up a telephone and began to dial.

"God only knows where we'll end up now," I said to Nila.

"You positive you understand where we want to go, Eidermann?" Nila said.

"Oh, yes, positive," Mr. Eidermann said.

"New York," Nila said. "United States of America."

"Yes, yes," Mr. Eidermann said. "Eidermann understands."

"In airplane," Nila told him. "Moscow to New York. Soviet Union to America. Direction from east to west."

"My dear lady," Eidermann said. "How many times I have to tell you that Eidermann understands?"

Someone tapped me on the shoulder. I turned around. It was the Italian spy. "Well, hello there," I said.

"You are going to America?" the spy said. "I think so," I said. "Can I speak to you in private?" the spy asked.

I followed him out to the corridor. He looked around

furtively and said, "You want to buy souvenir of your trip to Soviet Union?"

"What kind of souvenir?" I asked him.

"Genuine piece of Noah's Ark direct from Mount Ararat," he said.

"Let me look at it," I said. The spy drew back, shocked.

"You think a person carries genuine piece of Noah's Ark around in his pocket?" he said. "I keep it locked in hotel room. Also I have for sale very ancient Russian icon."

"How ancient?" I asked. He thought for a moment and then he said, "Tenth century."

"How much money do you want for it?" I asked. The spy said he would sell me the icon and the piece of Noah's Ark and throw in a bronze bust of Lenin in the bargain in a package deal. "All three valuable items in exchange for Polaroid camera," he told me.

"No," I said. "Not interested. Thanks anyway."

"Oh, well, I didn't expect you would," the spy said resignedly. "You have maybe some chewing gum?"

"I'm sorry, I don't," I said. The spy left. I went back into Mr. Eidermann's office.

"All arranged," Mr. Eidermann told me. "Two seats aboard Pan-American flight 94, Moscow to New York, leaving this evening."

Stanley picked me up at the hotel in the afternoon. "I'm going to take you to visit a kindergarten where the Russian children are taught to speak English," he told me. "I know the kindergarten manager."

The kindergarten was housed in an ornate pre-Revolutionary mansion that had once belonged to the Turkish embassy. There was a flower garden in the back yard. "The children plant the flowers and tend to them," Stanley told me.

There were swings and slides in the back yard, and a sandbox filled with white sand underneath the trees.

"Russian children attend kindergarten from the time they are three years old until they are seven," Stanley said. "Their parents have the choice of sending them to English-, French- or German-speaking kindergartens. Whichever language they choose is the language the child continues to study throughout its school years."

The cost to the parents is minimal, Stanley told me. Schooling in the Soviet Union is supported by the state. The children live at the kindergarten throughout the week and go home only on weekends.

"There are approximately twenty children in each class," Stanley said. "Each class has one teacher assigned to it in addition to another woman who is a combination housemother and supervisor. There are also music teachers, nurses, cooks, and other domestic personnel."

The kindergarten teacher greeted us warmly. She was a pleasant-faced woman carrying her year-old grandson in her arms.

"He is visiting me for the week," she told us, smiling. "My daughter says I spoil him but I tell her it is impossible to spoil such a good baby. We are honored to have an American lady visit with us. The children are tremendously excited. I thought it might be interesting for you to visit our class of four-year-olds today because the three-year-olds are only beginning to learn to speak English. Here is the room where the children sleep."

The high-ceilinged airy chamber was filled with rows of tiny cots. "The children make their own beds," the manager said, "and I am afraid they are not very good at it yet, but they try hard."

A series of diminutive lockers stood against the wall. The manager opened the door of one. Inside was a pair of small pink bedroom slippers. Above the lockers hung a series of watercolors depicting highlights in the lives of Goldilocks, Peter Rabbit, and Papa Lenin.

"And now come and meet our children," the manager said. Still carrying the baby, she led the way into what must have been the former ballroom of the embassy. A grand piano stood at one end of the room. The original gilt-framed, floor-to-ceiling mirrors still hung from the peeling walls.

"Our building is being modernized," the manager told us. "Unfortunately the work goes slowly because the authorities have so many more important priorities."

At her invitation Stanley and I sat down on two of the wooden kindergarten chairs. The music teacher struck a few chords on the piano and launched into a spirited march. The doors opened and the children filed in. They marched around the room once and formed a semicircle facing us.

The class consisted of about twenty boys and girls. The boys were wearing short pants and sweaters. The girls were dressed in crisp cotton frocks. Every face was scrubbed and shining.

One little girl whose pigtails were tied back with an enormous butterfly bow stepped forward and smiled at us shyly. She was wearing a red-and-white striped pinafore, a ruffled blouse, and red patent leather sandals with white ankle socks.

"Good afternoon," she said. Her English was halting

but perfectly enunciated. "We are happy you came to visit us from America. We will sing you a song. Thank you very much."

She stepped back. The teacher struck another chord on the piano and the children sang in chorus—

"We love our mother
"She works for us day and night
"We love our mother
"Her face is so kind and bright"—

"This is a song the children learn to sing for holiday on which we honor all Soviet mothers," the manager told us—

"We love our mother
"We know she loves us too
"We love our mother
"We love her, oh yes we do."

The song was over. Stanley and I applauded. All the little girls curtsied and the boys bowed. The teacher of the class beamed with pride. One of the cooks, who had tiptoed into the room to listen to the children sing, was beaming and applauding also.

The little girl stepped forward again and said, "Good afternoon. Now we will dance for you."

The music teacher struck up a gay polka and the children chose partners, although several of the boys had to be prodded into action by the teacher and the housemother. One small redheaded boy sat down in a corner and refused to budge. The rest of the children danced an enthusiastic polka, after which they lined up again in front of us, breathless and giggling.

Now it was a boy who stepped forward as spokesman for the class.

"We are very happy you could come to visit us," he

said. "We—we—" He was unable to remember what came next. His eyes filled with tears. The teacher hurried over and put her arms around him and whispered to him soothingly. The little boy nodded and wiped his eyes with the back of his hand.

"We want to give you gift to take back to America!" he went on, in a rush of words. With this he scampered out of the room and returned in a moment, clutching a sheaf of flowers from the children's garden.

"These are our own flowers," he said to me. "We grew them all by ourselves and now we would like to give them to the children of America."

He solemnly handed me the bouquet of flowers.

"Please tell the children of America that the children of Moscow send greetings to them from across the sea," the little boy said.

CHAPTER THIRTEEN

Peace to the huts; War upon the palaces!

Vladimir Ilich Ulanov

"Who this person supposed to be?" Moscow Customs Control demanded. He was looking at my passport photograph.

"That's me," I said. Customs Control examined the photograph through narrowed eyes. He stared at me suspiciously. "I had a haircut in Armenia," I explained.

Customs Control returned my passport and my very important documents and asked me whether I was carrying any gold, silver, or living relatives out of the Soviet Union.

"No," I said. He eyed my luggage as though he suspected me of smuggling Cousin Masha out in the hang-up garment bag but at last he opened the boarding gate and allowed us to pass through.

The path to the waiting Pan-American jet was lined with uniformed Soviet guards standing at stiff attention. Their faces were coldly expressionless. Their eyes stared straight ahead. It was a chilling farewell and I had to overcome an impulse to break into a panicky dash for the safety of the plane. Just as I was about to climb on board Nila said, "Wait!"

She turned to the purser who was standing at the foot of the boarding steps. "Tell me please," she said. "This airplane belongs to Pan American?"

"Yes, madam," the purser said. "Is flight number 94?" Nila asked. "Yes, madam," the purser said.

"Flies to New York?" Nila asked. "Of course, madam," the purser said.

"You are not planning to go on strike before plane lands in America?" Nila asked.

"Of course not, madam," the purser said.

"Go ahead," Nila told me. "Safe to get on board."

I climbed on the plane, still carrying the bouquet of flowers from the children of the Moscow kindergarten. As soon as I found my seat I asked the stewardess to put the flowers in water for me until we reached New York. Then I opened my passport case and took out all the very important Soviet documents and tore them up into little pieces.

"Kindly dispose of these little pieces of paper for me," I said to the purser.

"Certainly, madam," he said. I fastened my seat belt. With a roar of its jet engines the plane took off. When we were airborne I drew aside the window curtain and looked out for my last glimpse of the Russian countryside. The stewardess reappeared.

"It looks just like Michigan," I said.

"I beg your pardon?" the stewardess said.

"I'd like something to read," I said. "Do you have *Airport*?"

"I'm sorry, we don't," the stewardess said.

"Thank God," I said. "Do you ski?" The stewardess said yes, a little. "Avoid the Intermediate slope at Magic Mountain, Vermont," I told her. "It leads straight to Pyatigorsk."

She gave me an uneasy glance. "Do you want a pillow?" she said.

"I do not want a pillow," I said. "I do not want to sit down. I am an American. This soup is oversalted. I need a rod, line and hooks. Something rattles."

"I'll go and see what is rattling," the stewardess said. She left.

"Why you are babbling to that poor girl like a mad?" Nila said to me.

"Because I'm so happy," I said. I looked out the window again. The blue Gulf of Finland sparkled beneath us. "We're out from behind the Iron Curtain," I told Nila.

The stewardess reappeared with champagne. Nila and I each took a glass.

"I wish to propose toast," Nila said. "Let us drink to marvelous idea I have for trip you and I will take next summer." She raised her glass.

"To Siberia!" Nila said.

RUSSIAN IN A NUTSHELL

Au Revoir

Well, it's time I went home.
NU, MN'E pa-RA i-T'I DAW-ma.

You must visit us when you come to America.
vi dalzh-NI ab'i-ZA til-na nas na-v'i-ST'IT' kag-DA
vi BU-d'i-t'i va-M'E-r'i-k'i.

I can't find my passport.
n'i-ma-GU nay-T'I svoy PAS-port.

ARE YOU CARRYING ANY GOLD OR LIVING RELATIVES?

I've found it!
na-SHOL!

Good-bye.
da-s'vi-DA-n'i-ya.